NICE RECOVERY

Alice, I Think

Miss Smithers

Alice MacLeod: Realist at Last

Another Kind of Cowboy

Getting the Girl: A Guide to Private Investigation,
Surveillance and Cookery

NICE RECOVERY

SUSAN JUBY

VIKING
CANADA

VIKING CANADA

Published by the Penguin Group

Penguin Group (Canada), 90 Eglinton Avenue East, Suite 700, Toronto, Ontario, Canada M4P 2Y3
(a division of Pearson Canada Inc.)

Penguin Group (USA) Inc., 375 Hudson Street, New York, New York 10014, U.S.A.
Penguin Books Ltd, 80 Strand, London WC2R 0RL, England
Penguin Ireland, 25 St Stephen's Green, Dublin 2, Ireland (a division of Penguin Books Ltd)
Penguin Group (Australia), 250 Camberwell Road, Camberwell, Victoria 3124, Australia
(a division of Pearson Australia Group Pty Ltd)
Penguin Books India Pvt Ltd, 11 Community Centre, Panchsheel Park, New Delhi – 110 017, India
Penguin Group (NZ), 67 Apollo Drive, Rosedale, North Shore 0632, New Zealand
(a division of Pearson New Zealand Ltd)
Penguin Books (South Africa) (Pty) Ltd, 24 Sturdee Avenue, Rosebank, Johannesburg 2196, South Africa

Penguin Books Ltd, Registered Offices: 80 Strand, London WC2R 0RL, England

First published 2010

1 2 3 4 5 6 7 8 9 10   (RRD)

Author representation: Westwood Creative Artists
94 Harbord Street, Toronto, Ontario M5S 1G6

Excerpts from *The Natural History of Alcoholism Revisited* by George E. Vaillant, pages 22, 263, 268,
reprinted by permission of the publisher, Cambridge, Mass.: Harvard University Press,
copyright © 1983, 1995 by the President and Fellows of Harvard College.

Excerpt from *Tweak: Growing up on Methamphetamines* by Nic Sheff reprinted with the permission of
Atheneum Books for Young Readers, an imprint of Simon & Schuster Children's Publishing Division.
Copyright © 2008 Nicholas Sheff.

Manufactured in the U.S.A.

LIBRARY AND ARCHIVES CANADA CATALOGUING IN PUBLICATION

Juby, Susan, 1969–
Nice recovery / Susan Juby.

Includes bibliographical references.
ISBN 978-0-670-06917-0

1. Juby, Susan, 1969–. 2. Recovering alcoholics—Canada—Biography.
3. Recovering addicts—Canada—Biography. 4. Authors, Canadian
(English)—21st century—Biography. I. Title.

PS8569.U324Z472 2010   C813'.6   C2009-907030-8

Visit the Penguin Group (Canada) website at **www.penguin.ca**

Special and corporate bulk purchase rates available; please see
www.penguin.ca/corporatesales or call 1-800-810-3104, ext. 2477 or 2474

For everyone who has ever tried, and failed,
to learn to drink like a grown-up

"Recovery is for quitters."
—*overheard in meeting*

Preface

ADDICTION MEMOIRS have an odd reputation, and I find myself a little embarrassed to be writing one. Not because I am ashamed of being an alcoholic, or because fabulists have given the genre a bad name, but because there are a few things that make them tricky. So before I begin to tell you the story of my downfall, which was not of the epic but rather the badly bruising variety, I will state outright just how much truth and accuracy you can expect herein.

Just because I was a teenage alcoholic and have been in recovery for many years doesn't give me the right to tell anyone else's private business. That means that I've changed other people's names and details of their stories and combined or disguised their identities to protect their privacy. Also, this book is not about my family. It's not my job to go embarrassing them. I've done enough of that already.

Some timelines and specifics may be inaccurate in my stories and those of others. This is because I'm writing about a period during which I and my subjects spent considerable time in a blackout. It surprises me that people go to addiction memoirs looking for accuracy. It's like going to the Amnesia Society looking for detailed family histories. I'm also highly suspicious of any addiction memoir that describes in minute detail exactly what happened when. Addicts and alcoholics are notorious fabricators. Just be aware. In short, you might want to look to memoirs of teetotalling genealogists with photographic memories if perfect recall and accuracy is your bag.

Most twelve-step programs are based on a principle of anonymity. That means that members do not break their anonymity at the level of press, radio, and film. Or books. My discussion about my (or others') membership in any self-help programs will be kept general to respect these traditions. This book touches on twelve-step programs and what they entail, but if you want more information, each program has its own literature. It's very useful stuff, and if you're interested, I encourage you to read it.

What you can count on being accurate is the general trajectory of my drinking and using career (determinedly downward) and how that affected every part of my life when I wasn't drinking. I have invented no dead friends, possible homicides, or trips to Turkish prisons (or Turkish baths, for that matter).

The sad truth is that, as I think about embarking on this book, I worry about not being hard-core enough. This is not uncommon. Some people in recovery worry about that sort of thing a lot. Until they get over it. I was never a Blood or a Crip or a full patch member of the Hells Angels. Nor was I homeless or a prostitute. I did not use needles except to sew. I did, however, cheat extensively on my eye exam in an attempt to get cute reading glasses and consistently told the dentist that I flossed when I didn't. This is the sort of person you are dealing with. Some of the profiles of young people in recovery include more crime and street involvement. The reality is that it's all the same. If you scratch the surface of any alcoholic or addict, underneath the veneer we seem to have the same busted equipment for dealing with life. When we let go of our illusions, our denial, and our love affair with our substance of choice, many of us feel like brittle shells constructed of equal parts fear, self-loathing, and self-obsession. Whether a person is addicted to alcohol, pot, crystal meth, cocaine, or heroin, or most likely some combination of these, there always seems to be a gaping hole where the sense of self should be.

I and the people I spoke with for this book know what it is to be beaten within an inch of your life by an addiction, to see your waking hours filled with anxiety and obsession and to have an already tenuous self-esteem obliterated by your own self-destructive behaviour.

The other thing we know is what it's like to sober up as a young person (in my case, at twenty) and to stay sober over the long haul, a task that requires faith, courage, and epic quantities of assistance; it is a journey as fascinating as any a person can take.

The newly sober, especially those who are young, often resign themselves to lives of colourless monotony. It turns out that while the highs and lows aren't quite so reminiscent of *The Perfect Storm*, there is also less degradation and pain involved in being sober. It's a completely involving journey with limitless nuance and, best of all, possibility for actual and profound change.

If telling these stories about addiction and recovery helps one person, it will have been worth it. Just please don't sic the accuracy police on me. I've done the best I can with the tattered remnants of my abused memory.

I remember enough.

part I

DRINKY PANTS

1

Hate to Be You If I Were Me

I SOMETIMES IMAGINE my pre-drinking personality as a rich field just waiting for some mind-altering substance to come along so that my alcoholic self could sprout and flourish. But in my case it wasn't the first drink that took root. This was a bit disappointing, at least from a storytelling perspective, because when you enter recovery for alcoholism and/or drug addiction, everyone wants to know about your first drink. It's supposed to be spectacular and set the stage for the complete wreck you later became. In an ideal war story, the first drink should end with you falling down, throwing up, and, if at all possible, in prison for an armed robbery and attempted kidnapping committed during a blackout.

Unfortunately, I only dimly remember my first drink. This fits with the fact that I can't remember most of my childhood. When I tell my story, I usually just pick an early drinking experience that illustrates the fact that right from the beginning I had an unusual (by which I mean unusually enthusiastic and dramatic) reaction to alcohol. But when I really think about it, I recall two first drinks.

I took my first drink at a wedding. I was eight or nine. The wedding was held outdoors in the country and was one of those all-day affairs that slowly disintegrate into social anarchy and moral dissolution. The wedding started at eleven in the morning, and by nightfall there was no one really paying attention to us kids.

We marauded around like a group of short bandits with severe attention deficit disorder who couldn't decide what to steal first. The freedom was heady and a little dizzying.

We went charging past one of the guests' cars, an enormous panelled station wagon, and I noticed a pair of brown leather dress shoes protruding from underneath the front bumper. The shoes were attached to the feet of one of the guests at the wedding party. Contrary to appearances, he was neither working on the undercarriage of the car nor dead. He'd chosen that somewhat curious location to take a nap.

"Is he okay?" asked one of the kids.

"Sure. That's Mr. Ronson," said my cousin.

"What's he doing under the car?" asked the first, who was not a blood relative. Anyone from our genetic line knew exactly what the man was doing under the car.

"He's passed out," explained another of my cousins, with an air of infinite, unflappable world-weariness.

I was impressed with Mr. Ronson's resting place. There was something so final about it. Nothing was going to disturb him, unless of course someone started the car and ran him over. Mr. Ronson probably wasn't the drunkest person at the wedding, but he appeared to be the most peaceful. I'd already been in plenty of situations, especially social ones, that made me want to retreat under a car. It seemed that you needed to be an intoxicated adult to actually do it.

"Should we tell someone?" I asked.

"Nah," said one of the older kids. "He's happy where he is. Let's go get ourselves a drink."

The bartender originally stationed in the bar tent had disappeared some time ago and the rest of the adult party-goers who hadn't gone home or passed out had disappeared into the still, sultry night to talk and drink in little groups.

The tables in what had been the dining tent were covered with empty bottles and glasses. The plastic tablecloths were crusted with melted wax from the candles that had been jammed into Chianti bottles to lend a little class to the event.

"Here," said one of the older kids. He handed me a half-full wineglass.

I inspected it carefully.

"Go ahead. There aren't any butts in it."

The other kids, ranging in age from seven to twelve, stood watching solemnly. I had no real desire to try drinking, perhaps because of the spectacular results I'd seen it produce in some of the adults around me. But something about the restful aspect of those shoes poking out from under the car had captured my imagination.

I raised the glass to my lips and took a sip of wine, trying to ignore the lipstick marks on the rim. My eyes watered and my stomach churned as I drank it down.

"Cheers!" said one of the older kids. He poured the dregs from several glasses into one. He took a powerful swig and I could see him struggling not to vomit.

And that was it. My first drink, after which nothing much happened.

LUCKILY FOR STORYTELLING PURPOSES, the second drink had a better arc to it. Let me set the stage. As I moved out of childhood into adolescence, I was disappointed to discover that I wasn't socially gifted. This can be explained by a few crucial factors. First, I spent an inordinate amount of time wandering around in swamps imagining that I was a young, female Gerald Durrell. Second, as a kid I was happy to chat with anyone and tell them, in more detail than was wise or necessary, what I thought about almost any topic. Third, I expected the best of people.

In spite of the fact that I was socially delayed, I had some friends. Up the hill from our house lived a family with three young girls, one of whom was my age. At home I had three brothers. The oldest was five years my senior, the younger were six and seven years my junior, and I felt a bit marooned between them. My lack of female siblings caused me to romanticize the notion of sisterhood to a nearly pathological degree. I was obsessed with *Little Women*, and as soon as I met the sisters up the hill, I wanted to spend every moment possible at their house, pretending I was one of them. Giselle, Christina, and Denise's commitment to the world of make-believe was absolute. I was a hardbitten realist in comparison. They played elaborate games, some of which took entire days, including the Hungarian Bulgarian Good Guy Dance Contest, which involved making up routines to suit songs on their Mellow Moments eight-track while wearing unfortunately hued leotards. They'd devised a kidnapping game that involved sending elaborate ransom notes in a made-up language, loosely based on the sounds made by their chickens, and they did death-defying routines on a stick and rope. These performances were scored using the Olympic system.

Giselle, Christina, and Denise and their lovely French-Canadian mother welcomed me into their family. Giselle, who was my age, was like a charitable foundation of one. She very kindly overlooked the bossy and annoying qualities that caused other kids my age to avoid me. I loved the girls' intensely social world but was also aware of being the extra, the one-of-these-things-is-not-like-the-other.

When I wasn't peering into mud puddles in a swamp, lecturing adults and other kids on my opinions, or "chicken talking" with Giselle and her sisters, I read with the focus of someone breathing through a straw. My reading wasn't confined to books about sisters. I read anything I could get my hands on.

Looking back, I'd have to say that it may have been a mistake to use books as a guide to life. This is because books misled me about a few things. Thanks to warm-hearted stories like *Anne of Green Gables*, I expected to encounter kindred spirits on every corner, as well as gruff but caring old people. Rather than ridding the world of gritty books, book-banning advocates should pay more attention to banning sweet books that set up false expectations. More Brothers Grimm, less Trixie Belden!

Books hoodwinked me into believing a set of lies about what was and was not important in life. In books and in my family, having a good vocabulary was crucially important. When I went to school it turned out to be a serious liability. In books a lack of concern about clothes and personal appearance showed solid character. In school such unconcern spelled social disaster. In books knowing a lot about a lot of things, such as breeds of horses and varieties of pond scum, was admirable and likely to be rewarded. At school it pretty much guaranteed that everyone would think you were a show-off and a bore and would shun you. In books people were mostly nice, and the ones who weren't nice were easy to spot. In school villains were everywhere and they were well disguised.

Had it not been for the society of Giselle and her sisters, I would have been completely friendless. And the more trouble I had with people, other than Giselle and her sisters, the more twisted my personality got. I seemed to be afflicted with both shyness and overbearing confidence, a uniquely loathsome combination.

This, plus a haircut that rendered my gender indeterminate, caused most would-be peers to avoid me. The rest used me to work out their aggressions. The more I was bullied at school, the more my paranoia, self-consciousness, and self-centredness grew. In other words, my field grew ever more fertile. A few other hapless kids and I rotated in and out of the uncoveted position of "least popular." Even a short-lived transfer into Catholic school didn't help.

By the time I hit middle school, I was suffering from a case of school-induced post-traumatic stress disorder and felt nothing but despair about the future. For the first seven years of school, I'd tried to tell myself that every little cruelty or betrayal or instance of meanness was a mistake. But by the time I started middle school I was convinced: other people sucked and so, more importantly, did I. What I learned from kindergarten through grade six is that everything I'd thought I had going for me was, in fact, a handicap. By grade seven I knew that the only solution was to change everything.

The old blues guy Robert Johnson is said to have stood at the crossroads and sold his soul to the devil. Others have made similar pacts in a variety of locations, such as at the bedside of their first-born. If the devil had come strolling by our house the morning before I started grade seven at Chandler Park Middle School, I'd have hit him with as many offers as a used SUV dealer in a gas crisis. "My first-born? YOURS!" "That extra kidney I've got kicking around? TAKE IT!" But the devil didn't stop by, unless he was disguised as one of the mean girls who cruised the hallways like bull sharks. I was going to have to be the author and engineer of my own personal revolution.

That is why the morning of the first day of grade seven, for the first time in my life, I agonized over what to wear. In previous years, Giselle's mom had sewn Giselle and me matching dresses. They were usually flowered and ruffled and made long-legged, long-haired Giselle look like a cross between an angel and an advertisement for laundry detergent. I looked more like a young boy experimenting with his sister's clothes. This year I was going to strike out on my own, fashion-wise. But what to wear? I was too old for the orange jumpsuit with the pictures of cats and interesting burn holes from stray cigarette ashes. Maybe I could still fit into my suspender pants? No luck. I tried on and discarded everything in my closet. There must have been three entire outfits lying on the bed when I decided on jeans and a white turtleneck. Surely no one could be offended by jeans. Giselle and her sisters were getting a ride with their mom that first day, so I caught the bus, turning over my agenda in my mind.

The first thing I had to do was to get some more friends. There was safety in numbers. What I needed was one of those peer groups I was always hearing about. Giselle would, as always, slide effortlessly into the nice girl category. I needed my own group.

On that first day at middle school we were all in the same boat. Everyone was looking for somewhere to fit. But everyone also seemed to know how to meet people, what to say to them, where to stand, and what to do with their hands and face. I didn't have a clue. So the moment I entered Chandler Park Middle School, I began to study my classmates, who came from elementary schools all over town, as though they were exotic fauna in a zoo. It took me less than a day to figure out who was cool and who wasn't. The ability to detect such information seems to be encoded in the DNA of the average thirteen-year-old, even one as socially tone-deaf as I.

The popular kids were too far out of reach. I might be new to most of them, but they terrified me with their good looks, enthusiastic, positive behaviour, and normal, happy families who I suspected did healthy activities such as skiing and hiking together.

Next I assessed the jocks. I was reasonably athletic. A good horseback rider and a fast runner, especially when someone was after me. But there was a lot of overlap between the popular people and the jocks. Plus, the jocks had special jock clothes and shoes and I couldn't see going to all the trouble of finding those.

Giselle and the other nice girls were, well, nice enough. But they didn't seem like a natural fit either.

That's when I noticed the wild ones, the baby delinquents. They were the girls who'd already discovered makeup, most notably black eyeliner, and could wield a curling iron like a Jedi handles a light sabre to produce perfectly feathered hair. They were the boys trying on grade-seven smirks and oversized lumber jackets. The wild ones left school property at recess and lunch. They walked together in small dark knots toward an alley that bordered the playing field. Rumour had it they spent their time in that alley smoking cigarettes and even doing some other stuff. They talked in class, slept in class, and sometimes even got kicked out of class. Some were good-looking and some weren't, which meant that they had flexible standards (a real bonus, to my mind). By the end of the day, I'd decided that these were my people, or at least they could be if I played my cards right.

2

Just Add Alcohol

THE KEY to fitting into my intended new peer group was learning to look the part. To achieve this goal, I went to the local drugstore and purchased a stick of black eyeliner and a compact containing baby- and midnight-blue eye shadow. I knew better than to put the makeup on at home. My mother didn't wear cosmetics and didn't approve of young people who did. When I arrived at school the next morning, I headed straight for the washroom. There, my hand shaking, I applied my new liner. I drew a thick, unsteady line over my top eyelashes and coloured in a thin strip of flesh between my lower lashes and my eyeball. Then I added a generous amount of blue eye shadow: baby-blue on the lower lid and midnight in the crease, baby-blue to the brow. The effect was startling and immediate. My eyes nearly disappeared!

When I walked down the hallway with my new eye-look, people who'd never noticed me before stared. Giselle dropped her lunch bag but quickly recovered and told me it looked very nice. A few days later people stared even harder because one of my tear ducts got blocked and I developed an eye infection that caused that eye to weep uncontrollably. Still, I felt I was putting out the right signals.

It took a week or two for people to settle into their groups. A select few kids from my elementary school turned effortlessly popular. A few went jock. I was still waiting to be claimed.

I nearly passed out with relief when a girl named Darcy walked up to me at the bus stop as I waited there at the end of the second week. I knew who she was. She lived a few blocks from our house and had also gone to Lake Kathlyn Elementary, though she'd never paid any attention to me other than to laugh along with everyone else when people took bets on whether I was a boy or a girl. She'd joined the wild ones as soon as she hit Chandler Park.

"Hey," she said.

I was nervous and my eye infection hurt, but I was thrilled that she was talking to me.

"Want to come downtown?" she asked.

Would I! My god. This was it! My big chance!

I nodded and tried not to let on how excited I was. Social revolutionaries always play it cool.

During my first hour with Darcy, I saw more crimes committed than in my previous twelve years combined. Darcy had three key skills that I saw as essential to my personal revolution. She (a) knew her way around the arcade, (b) knew all the other wild kids, and (c) could shoplift up to three pairs of pants at a time.

I didn't realize what she had been doing in the clothing store we'd stopped at until we got to the arcade and went to the bathroom to attend to our eyeliner. She stood in front of the sink and unbuttoned pair after pair of jeans.

"Why," I asked, "did you wear so many pants to school?"

"I didn't wear them, you idiot," she said. "I lifted them. I can sell you a pair if you want. Give you a good deal."

I nodded uncertainly and immediately started planning how I'd explain new pants to my mother.

"Want a cigarette?" she asked.

Would I! I'd been waiting for the cigarettes to come out.

Obviously I'd picked exactly the right person to help me transform my life. Robert Johnson couldn't have had more luck with the devil. Moments later I was smoking my first cigarette.

After we finished smoking, Darcy led the way out of the bathroom. In the old arcade loitered most of the worst-behaved boys from middle school and even high school. A few of them were playing foosball with the kind of intensity varsity athletes bring to championship games. I began to sweat.

"Let's go talk to some guys," said Darcy, moving fearlessly toward them, as though approaching boys was the most natural thing in the world.

As we got closer, the boys looked at us, their dark eyes promising and threatening.

"Hey," said Darcy.

"Who's your friend?" asked a boy with spidery eyelashes and curly hair. I could see the top of a package of cigarettes poking out of his lumberjack shirt. The day before I'd seen him get kicked out of class for fooling around. He was extremely fine.

"Introduce yourself," Darcy instructed.

I smiled weakly but couldn't seem to make any words come out.

"Can't she talk?" asked the boy.

"Who knows?" said Darcy.

As quickly as it had appeared, the flicker of interest left the boy's eyes and I was once again left standing outside the circle of cool.

I left the arcade alone and walked over to my mom's office, quietly devastated that I'd blown my first real social opportunity. The next time, I vowed, I'd do better.

WHEN I WENT BACK to school the next day, I brought along some allowance money that I'd saved up for emergencies. I approached Darcy as she and her friends were leaving the school grounds to smoke their lunch.

"I brought money," I told her.

She stared.

"For the pants."

Suddenly she laughed. "Right on."

Ten minutes later I was wearing my new two-sizes-too-small jeans and I had an invitation to hang out with Darcy on Friday night. As I stiff-legged my way from class to class that afternoon, a few of the other wild girls nodded at me. I felt like a jewel thief who'd cracked a not very impregnable safe. I was in.

Now I just had to get over my fear of strange boys. My extreme shyness around boys was odd because I was able to speak to my brothers and even yell at them just fine. I suspect my mom instilled the fear in me as part of her campaign to keep me from getting pregnant. She wasn't a mentally ill fundamentalist, like Carrie's mom. She was more like a severely disillusioned sex-ed counsellor. She'd worked for years handing out social assistance to women who'd made the mistake of getting pregnant out of wedlock. Women who, in some cases, had made the same mistake five or six times with five or six different men.

Somehow my mother managed to convey to me the impression that pregnancy lurked around every corner, like an airborne infection. In defence of my mother, she never actually said this out loud. But I knew that's what she meant when she warned me to "be careful" who I hung out with.

She was also a fanatic on the subject of birth control. Any time the subject of boys and dating came up, she got terrifyingly *open*.

She encouraged me to tell her if I was about to have sex so she could get me some birth control. But she didn't say it in the calming way of sex education videos or in the hopeful way she used when encouraging my straight brothers to tell her if they thought they were gay. (She was always lobbying for one of them to go gay. As much as a pregnant daughter was a disaster in her mind, a gay son would have been a source of endless pride, probably because of the decreased risk of pregnancy associated with same-sex unions.) Her birth-control openness was tinged with depression and hopelessness. "For god's sake, before you do anything, just come to me and we'll get you some protection," she'd say. "Anything is better than that you get pregnant and end up like one of my clients." Her handling of the subject was perhaps the most effective form of birth control ever invented.

There was one other thing that caused me to be abnormally shy around boys—my reading material. Not the wholesome kind that gave me all the wrong ideas about people's essential niceness, but the other kind. When I was nine or ten, I discovered the stash of books my mom kept locked in her sewing room. One day when she was attempting to sew me a costume for a skating pageant, a traumatic process for both of us, she had to leave the room to answer the phone. I started snooping around her private library. That's when I found a copy of Henry Miller's *Sexus*. I snuck the book out of the sewing room and retreated to my room to read it.

What I learned from Henry Miller is that boys are sick. Really, really sick. They don't like women much and are interested in only one thing, which, as far as I could tell from my reading, was doing it doggy style, preferably while swearing at and secretly hating their sex partner. I read the dirty bits of *Sexus* over and over, letting the horror of Miller's attitudes toward women and sex seep into my subconscious. By the time I met the wild ones, I was too afraid of boys and their disgusting, pregnancy-inducing tendencies to even say hello. This would have been fine if the plan was to join a convent, but my social revolution involved the goal of turning into a boyfriend-having party girl *par excellence*. I had to figure out how to get over my shyness.

DARCY CELEBRATED the occasion of our first night out together by stealing us matching green-and-white-striped shirts, tight enough to show off our total lack of assets. We walked the mile or so into town along Highway 16 in our so-tight-they-hurt jeans. I'd gone over to Darcy's place, a tidy double-wide mobile home on a one-acre lot near the lake, to get ready. She'd helped me put on some purple eye shadow for a change of pace, and we both wore watermelon-flavoured Bonne Bell lip gloss and circles of pink rouge on our cheeks. The walk was long and the jeans were tight, but I was excited in a way I'd never been before. Every car that passed was a potential adventure. What if there was a rock star in one of them? Like Billy Idol, for instance, or Nick Rhodes. What if the lost rock star picked us up and gave us a ride and realized that we were extremely cool and took us on tour with him? In my mind, that was completely likely.

My mother had no idea where I was or what I was doing. She thought I was over at Darcy's simply hanging out. No one could have predicted this was the first of many, many walks to town for me.

As Darcy and I walked, slowly, due to the fit of our jeans, we talked about boys. Our blond hair, elaborately feathered, didn't move in the wind, thanks to generous applications of Aqua Net Extra Hold spray.

"I like John Emerson," said Darcy. "He's got nice eyes."

I nodded.

"Ken Vanderveen is hot, too," said Darcy.

I nodded again.

I didn't know any of the boys well enough to have strong opinions about them. In truth, my fear of getting pregnant or having to do disgusting sexual things meant I avoided even eye contact. But I felt I had to add something or she might get suspicious that I wasn't mature.

"I like Danno," I told her.

"Who?"

"You know. Danno. From *Hawaii Five-O.*"

Darcy stared like I'd just confessed that I had a crush on a Cabbage Patch doll or Mr. Dress-up.

"He has blond hair and brown eyes. That's the best combination," I explained, lamely.

A semi-trailer whooshed past, and I felt all my hair lift in one piece in the wake that followed. I breathed deeply of exhaust and waited for Darcy to say something.

"I meant someone real," said Darcy.

"Oh."

In my mind, Danno was real. I mean, I knew I couldn't date him because he was in his thirties and lived in Hawaii and was busy booking criminals, but he was real enough for me. Who knew when I might get over to Hawaii? If I did, I planned to bring a condom. Just in case.

When we finally reached Main Street, we only made it a block or so before we got picked up by a boy driving a small blue truck. He must have been from the high school. I'd never seen him before.

He leaned over and spoke through his open driver's side window.

"Hey, Darcy," he said. "There's a party at the gravel pit tonight. Want to check it out?"

"Right on," said Darcy.

We got into the little truck, which wheezed its way up Main Street and then back down, past the brick storefronts that housed the Post Office and most of the retail outlets in town. At the end of the street we headed down the highway toward the river. Black Sabbath rattled tinnily out of the cheap stereo and made the truck's windows vibrate. The town looked completely different from the passenger seat of a strange boy's truck. Beside me sat my new friend who stole pants. My personal revolution had moved into overdrive, I thought with satisfaction.

At the gravel pit there were only a few dirt bikes parked to the side of a small, nearly invisible fire flickering in the bright early evening. A group of high school boys stood around the flame. One of them caught my eye. He had curly blond hair and brown eyes. He looked like a younger version of Danno.

"Do you know those guys?" Darcy asked our driver as we sat in the parked truck.

"Nah," he said. "Not really."

No one spoke for a long minute. The driver pulled a plastic mickey of rum from somewhere deep inside his pants.

"Drink?" he asked.

"Right on," said Darcy.

The boy handed her the bottle, and she took a deep swallow, gasped once, wiped her mouth with the back of her hand, and handed it back. He wiggled the mickey in front of me like it was herring and I was a starving halibut.

"Want some?"

I looked at the boys outside and this boy inside. I grabbed the bottle and drank. It burned going down and settled uneasily in my stomach like a sick snake. I drank again.

We passed the bottle between us until it was gone. I've always wondered how other people experience alcohol, how their bodies interact with it, and how they feel after a few drinks. I'll tell you how I felt. Like I'd just been cast in the next John Hughes movie as the quirky but adorable female lead, who had coincidentally just been accepted to Harvard on a full scholarship and had recently won a gold medal in a popular sport. I felt lucky. Invincible. Powerful. A few drinks drowned all the fear and anxiety that rang constantly in my ears and blurred my vision. A few drinks turned me so outlandishly confident, exuberant, even, that I had to share the excellence that was me. The little truck could not contain me.

This explains why moments after we finished the bottle I was striding across the gravel pit toward the group of boys, Darcy running after me in the peculiar gait caused by the very tight pants.

"You!" I barked at the boy with the curly hair as I marched up to him. "You look like Danno!"

I stared at him, trying to decide whether to hug him, kiss him, or put him in a headlock.

He grinned nervously at his friends.

"Danno's hot," I told him. "He can book me anytime. And so can you." Then I winked, using my non-infected eye.

The rest of the boys standing around in the circle laughed— approvingly, it seemed to me.

"You ever hear of ZZ Top?" I demanded.

The blond boy shrugged and gave a hesitant nod.

"You know that song, 'Sharp Dressed Man'? Well, that's you."

The blond boy blushed and looked down at his shirt. He had on a mud-splattered dirt-biking jersey.

I began to sing, putting a lot of feeling into it. I'd gotten out the first couple of lines and was beginning to do the ZZ Top shuffle when Darcy started dragging me away.

I was still singing as Darcy pushed me back into the truck.

"Go," she told the driver. "Go!"

As we pulled out, I leaned over Darcy and out the window to belt out a few lines from "Legs," my other favourite ZZ Top song. The last I saw of them, the boys in the gravel pit were doubled over with laughter.

"You're crazy," breathed Darcy. She sounded impressed.

The boy in the driver's seat glanced over at me, an appraising look in his eye, and said, "I think *you* should have another drink."

I nodded decisively. "I guess I *am* crazy. And I guess I *will* have another drink."

The next thing I remember was waking up at home the next morning. I'd been sick next to my bed. I felt like someone had scooped out my insides, let them rot for a while in the hot sun, and then put them back. My brain was fevered and images of my performance at the gravel pit flashed before my eyes, causing searing embarrassment. The cure for shyness was also the disease. I knew one thing: I would never, ever get drunk like that again.

3

Flashdance and the Leg Warmer Blues

AS SOON AS MY HANGOVER FADED, so did my resolve to never drink again. In fact, the nausea and shame were hip-checked out of the way by a burning desire to try again. I'd loved the feeling of being confident and unselfconscious, even for a few minutes. It was as though alcohol gave me the break from myself that I'd been craving. For years I'd felt as though I was allergic to myself: alcohol was my EpiPen. Now all I needed was to learn how to drink properly. Luckily, drinking was a core activity among my new friends. We stole booze from our parents and mixed it together in Mason jars to create noxious but powerful potions that we drank out in the woods. Then we would stagger around and sometimes throw up. And after each episode, I'd find myself sick to death and humiliated, even if I hadn't done any singing or dancing or even much talking, which always got me into trouble. I suffered remorse of the damned every time I drank but it lasted only as long as the hangover.

In some cultures adolescents come of age in well-established ceremonies. They take sojourns in the wilderness or undergo purification rituals involving corporal punishment. In my town, as in many Western societies, one prime coming-of-age ritual was to host a drinking party. Soon after I became a card-carrying member of the party nation, my friends and I decided we were ready to graduate from staggering around in the bush by ourselves to staggering around with other people in a house. Being precocious in all things related to partying, my wild friend Darcy decided she wanted to have a party at her house. She had an older brother, which meant we had ready access to alcohol. We were set.

She invited us over to her place on a Friday night when she knew her parents would be out. It was to be my first real party, meaning one with older boys, drugs, and booze, and I was entirely, one hundred percent stoked. The fact that it was going to be held at the home of my new friend made me feel that great things were possible and even likely.

At this point, I wasn't completely sure what would constitute a great thing. A lot of beer was a great thing and so was weed. The possibility of getting a boyfriend was perhaps the greatest thing of all. The minute I picked up my first drink I jettisoned childish dreams of becoming a doctor or an astronaut or even a Zamboni driver. Instead I aspired to be like some of the tough older girls I saw who dated men who drove trucks or to be like the lead character in *Flashdance*. The movie had recently hit the theatres and, like almost every other girl (and quite a few guys) who saw it, I became obsessed with dancing like Jennifer Beals (or to be strictly accurate, Beals's stand-in). Not that I practised dancing or anything. I wanted to wake up one day and discover that extreme dance ability had descended on me from above. The idea of being the hot, misunderstood quasi-stripper who was also a welder was exciting. Somewhere along the line I decided that what a person needed to dance like Jennifer Beals was leg warmers. I surmised that nice warm calves were what enabled her to perform the essential moves, including peeling off the (in my case unnecessary) bra without removing the off-the-shoulder sweatshirt, and pulling a chain to unleash the torrent of water onto one's head while seated in the middle of an empty but nicely lit stage.

When I heard about the party, I was nervous, as always when faced with a social situation. I knew that I could get loaded at the party and that would take care of my nerves. But what about the four or five days between the announcement and the party itself? I decided a new article of clothing would get me through the rough patch. So I went to the local jeans store and was thrilled to find they'd begun to carry leg warmers. I was in such a hurry to get a pair that I didn't even wait for Darcy to steal them and instead paid full price.

They were light grey, machine-knitted, acrylic tubes, and when I put them on over my jeans they made my lower legs look like those of a juvenile elephant with water retention issues. They also made me feel capable of breaking into an extremely demanding dance routine at a moment's notice, though not while I was sober, obviously. Dancing, even with leg warmers, was best left until after I'd had a few drinks and was ready for my inner flashdancer to emerge.

After an hour and a half of intense curling iron work to get my hair to feather so that it met at the back like two buttocks coming together, and elaborate full-coverage application of black eyeliner and blusher and concealer, I was ready to face my public at the house party. Maybe that motocross guy who looked like Danno would be there!

Off I went, down the lake road toward Darcy's house in all my leg-warmed glory. It was not quite five o'clock in the afternoon. We were too young to party at a more fashionable hour. My mother wasn't home from work yet, so she wasn't there to stop me or ask any inconvenient questions about where I was going.

I was the first guest to arrive. Darcy and I sat on her front steps, the ones her father had built out of plywood and pushed up against the trailer to serve as a porch. We smoked Player's Light cigarettes and shared a Mason jar full of Sambuca, Malibu, Crown Royal, gin, and vermouth. It knocked me into a stuttering blackout almost immediately. At some point, we were joined by many of the other middle school wild ones. It was still light outside. I was pleased to see that I was the only one wearing leg warmers. We turned on the record player and danced. And when we finished, it seemed that the trailer had magically filled up with boys. High school boys. Darcy's brother's friends. They were dressed in lumber jackets and smelled like pot and they carried cases of beer.

By this time, my confidence had kicked in. It wasn't just the alcohol and the weed. The leg warmers had done something to my sense of personal importance. In addition to bestowing upon me the power of dance, *those leg warmers seemed to have given me the longed-for gift of gymnastics!* When I wasn't dreaming about having an older boyfriend and being a terrific dancer, I had fantasies in which I was an immensely talented gymnast who could perform death-defying tumble routines. This in spite of the fact that, even as a toddler, I had never been able to touch my toes.

I swanned around the party, feeling Beals-erized and lithe. Cutting-edge and limber. In truth, I was hammered beyond all hope of redemption.

It didn't take me long to figure out that someone besides me was admiring my action. He was, I thought, the best looking of the older guys at the party, stocky, with a handsome, lightly freckled face. His teeth were straight. At that time my teeth were trussed up like unruly mental patients in order to cure my overbite, so I always took note when people had nice teeth.

My recollection of our conversation is fuzzy. I think it went something like this:

Him: Hey. Nice leg warmers.

Me: Thanks.

Him: Want a beer?

Me: Yes.

A pause as he watched me guzzle the beer in a very welder-ish fashion.

Him: Hey, why don't you come with me for a minute?

Me and my leg warmers followed the handsome older boy to my friend's bedroom.

Considering that I was already a committed drinker and had been for a few months, I was also still kind of naïve. I knew that it probably wasn't an excellent idea to disappear into a room with a boy I'd only just met. I assumed he would try to kiss me and that would be a good thing. Because then he'd be my boyfriend and I would be the first leg-warmer wearer in grade seven who was dating a high school man.

Sweet!

So I happily kissed him on my friend's small, unmade bed. But then he did something strange. He pushed me off the bed in front of him. I thought maybe he'd dropped something and needed me to help him find it. I was glad I had my leg warmers on, but also a little worried that they might get dirty. My friend's room was a sty. There were clothes and tapes and stuff all over the floor.

Then he stood in front of me and pulled down his pants.

I gaped at him in astonishment.

This was even worse than Henry Miller had led me to believe! In my drunken state, I struggled to think through my options. I didn't want to be rude or embarrass him by saying no, even though what he seemed to be proposing was very, very low on my list of things I wanted to do. Probably just a few spots below "Cut off finger with rusty axe" and "Fall down and break arm in three places so the bone protrudes through the skin." I tried to gather my thoughts. My stomach, however, couldn't wait for me to come up with excuses.

The lethal mixture of booze and dope, dancing and smoking and unexpected pantslessness was too much and before I could warn him, I'd thrown up all over his footwear and legs. Like a threatened squid, my body had released the perfect defensive diversion.

"Oh man!" he said. "Are you puking?"

"No," I said, staring at the vomit dripping down his front.

"Fuck," he said, staring down at himself with his hands in the air. "Gross!"

And that's pretty much all I remember from my first house party and what was, technically speaking, my first date. I woke up the next day, sick with remorse and shame and the realization that quitting drinking wasn't just a good idea, it was a complete and total necessity. I wasn't the only one who had an early drinking experience like that. In fact, my experience was relatively mild. I kept hearing about girls going to parties, getting drunk, passing out, and waking up to find strange boys having sex with them. People whispered about these events and the people involved. The blame floated around, waiting to be assigned.

That evening was also the first in a series of notable vomiting incidents, something for which I became quite famous, especially after a projectile puking episode that occurred at my first concert (Trooper at the Civic Centre). In that case I nearly hit the band from one of the top bleachers. But I digress.

The party also marked the beginning of a shift in my relations with the wild ones. The next Monday at school Darcy walked up to where I was standing with some other girls who'd been at the party.

"Did someone get sick in my room?" she asked, staring at me.

"Uh, no," I said. I was pretty sure most of the barf ended up on the guy rather than the carpet or bed, so that was a little bit true.

"My parents smelled it," she said. "And now I'm in trouble."

"Oh," I said.

"I hate liars," she continued, still staring at me. The other girls nodded in agreement. "And sluts," she added.

When they walked away, I was left with a feeling that my life was spinning out of control. The blame for this one was landing square on me. I realized that none of it would have happened if I hadn't been drunk. The only solution was to quit drinking for real this time. Or at least work harder at learning to drink properly.

4

Some Bad News about
Your Lower Companions

THERE ARE STAGES to blowing up your life, even when your life is still pretty new and doesn't have a lot of square footage to be destroyed. I was methodical about how I obliterated my old self in the same way that a stick of dynamite is methodical. Okay, methodical is the wrong term. I was thorough. Let's put it that way.

Along with airborne pregnancy, another thing my mother warned me about was a class of people she called "bad news." We'd be talking about the kid down the road, the one with the limp and the motorcycle that got pushed more than ridden. "Oh, him," she'd say. "He's bad news." As though the kid were a piece of correspondence dipped in something foul and contagious; the human embodiment of doom. I thought it would be the worst possible thing to be labelled bad news. Once you were bad news in my mom's books, you weren't worth the motorcycle you pushed over, as my older brother discovered when he began to hang out with a couple of guys my mother didn't like. Her laments against some of his friends were prolonged, enthusiastic, and often loud. But my older brother has integrity. He hung out with whomever he wanted, no matter what kind of news they were. He remained friends with people for life. And my mother got over her concerns.

I, on the other hand, was made of weak and easily influenced stuff. Once my mother suggested someone was bad news I couldn't forget it for even one second. As I began my revolution I was terribly bothered by the knowledge that Darcy and most of my new wild friends seemed to be the bad news my mother had warned me about. Something in me protested against the idea that I was now on the bad-news team. Sure, "out-of-control, possibly slutty teen with a drinking problem" seemed to be my new identity, but that wasn't quite the same as being bad news, was it?

Oddly, the more I worried that my friends were bad news, the more I tried to prove to them that I was as bad as they, if not worse, the same way that I pretended to have poor grammar around people with poor grammar. I felt like if I behaved badly, then they wouldn't feel so bad about themselves.

The truth is that I was more than a little scared of the stealing and violence that marked my friends' progress through middle school. In fact, I was more than a little scared of *them*. I was too nervous to do crime and not a good fighter, so I tried to fit in by acting like an ass in school and by drinking.

Convincing my teachers at middle school that I was a rotten egg wasn't difficult. They didn't know about all the academic awards I got in elementary school. All they saw was my increasingly disruptive behaviour and all they heard was my foul language.

Swearing was the foundation stone of my attempt to gain middle-school street cred. "Fuck off," I'd say when another girl asked if I had the homework from Mrs. Whatever's class. "Eat shit," I'd say in the pause where other people might use "No way?" or "Really?" The problem was that I had extremely bad timing. The vice-principal of the school, a man you'd think I would have noticed occasionally given that he was approximately eight feet tall, always seemed to be hovering nearby when I used my swears. I'd come out with a stream of the foulest language I could muster and would be waiting for my classmates to giggle at my hilarious potty mouth and a second later a voice would boom from just over my left shoulder.

"Ms. Juby! Do you use that foul language at home?"

Shame would swamp my shallow vessel and I'd slink off. Only kids who were bad news got caught swearing in front of the vice-principal, Mr. Dundurn. And even though I was doing my best to fit in with the bad newsers, I didn't want to actually be one. The wild ones, though, loved my schtick unreservedly. They thought my swearing and my total inability to get away with swearing was the funniest thing ever. It even made up for my rumoured sluttiness and tendency to barf. At least for a while.

The thing was, I *did* use that language at home. We all did. One time, my older brother thought it would be amusing to teach my youngest brother some swear words. That was fine when it was just us kids, but then came the day my mother was pushing my youngest brother, who was three or four at the time, around the supermarket. My youngest brother was a taciturn child, and he often wore a stern look on his face that was unusual on such a small kid. His severe expression caught people's attention and caused them to condescend to him even more than they would to a regular, smiley child. On this visit, the produce man came over and, using his best sing-song, talking-to-a-baby voice, said, "And do you like fruit, young man?" To which my youngest brother, scowl firmly in place, replied, "Fuck off, cocksucker."

So in a way, swearing was part of a family tradition.

The day I got suspended for the first time it wasn't for drinking or swearing, but was related to the overhaul that my standards were undergoing at the time. I'd become a serious and, I thought, seriously stylish smoker almost right away. I blew my first fully formed smoke ring in the first week. At first I hid my smoking from my mother (who remained unaware of it for a while because she was so saturated in cigarette smoke herself it was impossible for her to smell the evidence), and I spent long hours smoking with other wild ones in various wooded locations, as well as little-travelled alleys and unused parking lots.

Then I got the bright idea that it would be less work to smoke just off school property. I was always in favour of anything that saved walking. I started smoking at the far edge of the play-ing field and convinced some of my friends to join me. The playing field was more or less directly in view of Mr. Dundurn's office, which, unfortunately for us, was equipped with windows.

He spotted me acting suspiciously, hauled me into his office, intimidated a confession out of me, and promptly suspended me. My memory here is a bit shaky, but I think he also suspended some other people. Word spread that I was an informer. As the Beat Up Susan Juby movement gained steam so did the impetus to change friends. But who would have me now that I was bad news, or at least so-so news?

That's when I noticed Charmagne, Nan, and Brenda. They were three of the prettiest girls in school and they always seemed to be laughing (in a condition my mom used to describe as "spinny") and were several orders of magnitude less scary than the wild girls. They did sports, but not too seriously, and were popular with almost everyone, including the good kids, the wild ones, and the jocks. I'd seen them at a couple of parties, and they definitely weren't opposed to having a good time.

I can't remember how I went about ingratiating myself with them. The lines between social groups weren't as hard and fast in middle school as they became in high school. To fit in with them

I tried to tone down the eyeliner use, wear jeans that were one size larger, and work on my jokes. Keeping them laughing was key.

We started doing things together and hanging out a bit after school. They enjoyed drinking nearly as much as I did, but weren't as into violence as the tougher wild ones.

My partial defection from the wild ones didn't go unnoticed. There were hostile mumblings from Darcy and her friends, but nothing too serious. I was partly shielded by my new friends. Then came the day the leader of my new friends, Charmagne, who had a full head of glossy brown hair and blue eyes with startling light grey flecks in the irises, came to school with some news.

"You want to go to the show this weekend?" I asked her. This was code for do you want to meet before a movie, get drunk, then wander around town mooning at boys until your parents come to get you.

"I can't," she mumbled. There was something strange in her voice.

"Why?"

"My parents said."

"You're not allowed to go to movies any more?"

Nan and Brenda wouldn't look at me.

"What?" I asked again, even though I was beginning to sense that I wasn't going to like the answer.

"The problem isn't the movies," she said.

"So ... what is it?"

"It's you," she said.

It was like a burning spotlight had come to rest on me.

"What about me?"

"Mr. Dundurn talked to them at the parent–teacher meeting last night."

"About me?" I repeated, unable to stop myself.

"Yeah. He said you're, you know, bad." Charmagne twirled a lock of hair around her finger and wouldn't meet my eye.

"What? Are you kidding?"

"He said you're evil," said Charmagne, whose parents were deeply religious.

The others nodded.

"He talked to your parents, too?" I asked Nan and Brenda.

"My mom was worried about my grades," explained Nan.

"Your grades are my fault?"

"They did kind of get worse after you started, you know, hanging out with us," she said.

Hot tears burned my eyes. I couldn't breathe.

My new friends walked away.

I didn't follow them. The worst thing was that part of me knew the vice-principal was right. I was bad news. I'd known it as soon as I had my first drink. It was like someone had just taken a big piece of my sense of self and thrown it away.

Charmagne, Nan, and Brenda and I were apart for only a few days. My mother called the school to complain when I told her what the vice-principal had said about me. But the hole that had opened up inside me remained. It was as though Mr. Dundurn had made my greatest fear real by speaking it out loud. I was not just bad news. I was bad. I was under attack from every direction. The negative external and internal messages I was getting, some intentional, some not, convinced me that I had a lot to hide. Not just the things that happened when I got drunk (most of which I didn't remember), but also the fact there was something fundamentally wrong with me. I was the imminent asteroid, the dirty bomb headed for your hometown. As a result of this awareness, when I was sober

I kept myself tightly controlled. I knew I had to work harder than anyone else to keep my mask on. It was crucially important that my clothes matched and that my makeup was just right and that I never showed any vulnerability. Any problem on the outside and the ugliness on the inside might be revealed for all to see. That, I thought, could kill me. The more match-y and controlled I got when sober, the more I started to explode when I drank and got high. And that was the worst news of all.

5

Second Prize

THERE WERE A FEW THINGS that kept me from falling apart as soon as I started drinking. One was my mother's rules. She had many and as much as I protested them, they gave structure to my life. Also, every time I missed curfew or lied about where I was and who I was with, I spent anywhere from two weeks to a month grounded. My mother never confronted me about why I was getting into trouble. Nor did the parents of anyone I knew, even if the kid was found covered in vomit on the front porch every Friday and Saturday night. We were just assumed to be going through our teen phase. And some of us were. Others, however, had jumped the rails and were headed down a whole other path, one that wasn't age specific.

I resented being grounded with every molecule of my being, but the enforced time out allowed me to recuperate, at least physically. Mentally, I was tortured by the thought of all the fun I was missing. I spent hour after hour listening to Nazareth's "Love Hurts" while lying on the couch in the living room with the drapes pulled. My groundings were nearly as painful for my family as they were for me.

The other thing that kept me from hitting the skids and dropping out of school as soon as I started drinking was my hobbies. They were legion. My mother instigated many of my activities, perhaps because she intuited I was going to need distractions in my life. I took piano lessons (briefly), went to Brownies (briefly), bowled, figure-skated, and sucked the big one at ballet. I attended 4-H and Saddle Club (our town's precursor to Pony Club) and in addition to reading, I loved to write. That's not to say that I was a prodigy or particularly talented. I wrote because I thought being a writer was glamorous and important and because it got me attention from teachers.

My first novel was completed sometime near the end of grade two. It was a timeless narrative about a girl who takes her dog to Mars via homemade spaceship. The most memorable thing about that story, which I wrote after school and during recess and lunch, was how much it impressed everyone.

As the stack of pages covered with misshapen capital letters grew, teachers dropped by my desk to marvel at the young Dostoyevsky in their midst.

"My goodness," they'd say. "Aren't you impressive!"

That was my cue to pretend to be so caught up in the creative process that I didn't even hear them.

"Looks like we've got a real writer on our hands!" they'd say.

At that I might allow myself a humble shrug of the kind Hemingway probably used when being complimented by his early mentors.

As far as I was concerned in the academic glory days of grade three, my teachers were right on all counts. I too was quite impressed with myself and my potential for greatness.

I was still writing and for pretty much the same reasons when I got to grade seven. My new specialty was stories about being misunderstood. Many of my works ended with the suicide of the main character, a figure of some genius who bore an uncanny resemblance to, well, me.

On the strength of this body of work, when I got to middle school, I was asked to compete in a local story contest by an English teacher, who was, like all good English teachers, extra nice to kids who read, even ones who were constantly in trouble, like me. He knew I was a writer, even though I hid it from some of my new friends, who didn't approve. He'd read some of my works and been encouraging.

"Very strongly felt," he wrote at the back of the piece about the girl whose parents were so cruel and insensitive about her social life that they, in the tradition of South American dictators, imposed a curfew, which left the girl no option but to throw herself off a bridge.

The story was made up of at least forty percent adjectives. On the back the teacher wrote, "Wow! Powerful stuff!"

My writing began to taper off almost as soon as I started drinking. I don't know why. It was like every time I drank, my mind got a little smaller. I could almost feel it happening. The channels that fed my imaginative landscape were pinched off, and I was left with a bonsai-ed set of real world concerns that included never missing a party, getting my hair right, and finding a steady bootlegger in the form of an of-age boyfriend with his own wheels. None of it seemed like anything anyone else would want to read about.

I don't know if my English teacher had picked up on the constricting trend going on in my brain, but he asked me to stay behind one day after school.

I did so, reluctantly.

"So, Susan," he said. "Are you going to enter the writing competition?"

As usual, I hadn't been paying attention in class, so I didn't know what he was talking about.

"Competition?"

"The one I've been announcing for the past three weeks? Sponsored by the local bookstore? Please tell me some of this rings a bell."

He saw from my blank expression that it didn't.

"Let me repeat myself while I've got your undivided attention. The competition is for promising young writers. To enter, you need to write a three-thousand-word story about the future."

"The future?" I said.

"You know, that thing that will happen later."

"Oh. That."

Other than standard homework assignments and tests, this was the first time a teacher had asked me to contribute anything since I'd turned my new, rotten leaf. I couldn't blow the request off. Obviously, I didn't have shit-all to say about the future, other than I hoped it involved getting very, very wasted. But some small part of me was hanging on to the child-writer gig.

The night before the piece was due, I sat down to write it. It had been a while since I'd written a story, and it felt awkward even to hold the pen. I tried to summon some deep, dark feelings. They ended up being a little too dark and possibly a little too real. They included the new sense that I was caught up in something I couldn't see through or over. The feeling had grown stronger after I tried to go a whole week without drinking and couldn't. I was beginning to feel like I had to drink or stay home in bed for the rest of my life. I was also assailed by the creeping awareness that the only thing I cared about without reservation was getting obliterated. I spent my sober hours filled with a vicious self-loathing that only getting loaded on alcohol could quiet. None of that seemed quite right for my story about the future.

So I picked a topic that scared me considerably less. I wrote an overwrought, vaguely imagined story about a nuclear holocaust survivor who walks along contemplating the destruction of the world. It seemed safer, plus I figured I'd get points for being political.

The story was a piece of shit and I knew it. That's why I was so surprised when my teacher announced the winners of the competition the following Friday.

First place went to a local lawyer's daughter, who belonged to a class of girls I thought of as "bubble gummers" because they were (to my mind) bright, shiny, sweet, and slightly sticky. What I knew about the winner from walking past her in the hall was that she enjoyed reading *The Economist* and not bothering much about her hair. (This was anathema to me, as I spent at least one hour every morning on my hair. Along with drinking to excess, my hair was my avocation.)

The winner's triumphant performance in the short story competition made perfect sense. She and the other bubble gummers were born to win. I, on the other hand ... not so much.

"And second prize goes to Susan Juby!" said the teacher, with a sad little note of hope in his voice, like that of a prison chaplain signing up a born-to-lose prisoner for choir duty.

Heads jerked up all over the classroom, including mine.

A couple of people elbowed each other. I felt an immediate surge of guilt. The story had taken about half an hour to compose. It was terrible. Either I got second place out of pity or only two people entered.

And still ...

"You girls can go by the store to pick up your prizes," said our teacher. The first-place winner carefully avoided looking at me. Having me in second place probably tainted the experience a bit.

I rolled my eyes at a couple of people to show I didn't care about any of it. Charmagne and Brenda and Nan had recently taken me back, partly because I made them laugh and partly because my behaviour while drinking was so extreme that they could get away with just about anything if I was around. I was once again hovering between them and the wild ones.

After school, Charmagne and Nan and I were walking downtown when a boxy green Volvo pulled up alongside us.

My breath caught in my throat. I knew the car. It belonged to a friend of the boy from the party. The one I'd thrown up on. I stared over the hood of the car at the dark blue mountain that loomed over the town so I wouldn't have to look inside.

"You girls need a ride?" asked a boy in the passenger seat.

Charmagne and Nan giggled and said sure. I followed my friends into the car. Jack the Ripper could have been in that car and I'd have followed them in. Once I was seated, I forced myself to look around. The boy wasn't there and I let out a huge sigh of relief.

The driver, a guy named Charles, famous for his commitment to getting baked, and his friend Aldous drove us halfway up the ski hill. They showed us how to "hotbox" a car. We smoked two joints without cracking a window until death via smoke inhalation seemed like a real possibility. Somehow, in the heavy white smoke, coughs, and muffled giggles, the seating arrangements changed and I found myself sitting next to Aldous, who'd been in the passenger seat. Charmagne and Nan moved into the front. They giggled every time Charles opened his mouth and some Spicoli-ism spilled out.

"Hey," whispered Aldous. He was solid and quiet and had thick brown hair that reminded me of a carpet.

I was panic stricken. Pot didn't relieve me of the burden of consciousness the way booze did. It just made me paranoid. More paranoid.

"That wasn't cool," said Aldous.

I turned to look at him. I could practically feel the blood vessels exploding in my eyes.

"What wasn't?"

"What he did to you," he said.

We both knew what he meant.

"Oh," I said. "I guess not."

At that moment a sludgy awareness came over me that the story of what had happened in that bedroom had been told and retold so it was now quite a bit worse for me.

I also realized that Aldous, by expressing solidarity, was being chivalrous, and I was bound by the rules of duty to be grateful to him.

"You want to sit on my knee?" he asked.

We had plenty of room in the back seat by ourselves.

"That's okay. But, uh, thanks anyway."

We sat in silence for a while. Then he grabbed my hand. I let him.

"We're going to go to the liquor store later. We found a guy to buy for us."

I felt the familiar flood of anticipation. Relief was on the way.

"I need to get something first," I said.

"From where?"

"The bookstore. I have to pick something up."

Aldous leaned forward and shoved Charles in the shoulder.

"Hey, we need to stop at the bookstore."

"Dude, I didn't know you could even fucking read," said Charles. Everyone, including me, laughed like this was the sharpest line of comedy ever spoken.

Several minutes later the driver pulled the car over in front of the bookstore on Main Street. I opened my door and emerged in a cloud of billowing smoke, like an extra in a Poison video. This earned me surprised and disapproving looks from everyone within sight and smelling distance.

"Back in a second," I said to no one.

I spent a long and painfully self-conscious moment standing outside on the sidewalk, in the hopes that my dope-saturated clothing would miraculously air out so I wouldn't be so conspicuous. Finally, I took a deep gulp of air and went inside. The store was filled with that quiet sense of purpose that a lot of books bring to a room. This made me feel even worse. Much as I loved books, had always loved books, I felt horribly out of place. Everyone here was so … not high.

The thought of going up to the counter and asking for my second-place prize was excruciating. I could already see the look I'd get from the guy behind the counter. Sure, he had a pleasant face. But the minute he saw my red eyes and smelled my eau de inside-of-a-bong perfume, he'd know I didn't deserve second prize in any writing contest, not even one that only two people had entered.

I was just on the verge of turning and leaving, when he called to me. "Can I help you?"

"I, uh," I said, with my usual pot-induced loquaciousness. Marijuana had precisely the opposite effect on me that alcohol did. When I drank I couldn't shut up. When I got high I was lucky to put together two words.

"Oh, hey! I bet you're one of our contest winners."

I flinched. Winner. It was not a word I associated with myself.

"Second prize," I muttered.

"Right on," said the man. He seemed unfazed by my inferior status. "You wrote a good story. Your prize is right here."

He reached under the counter and pulled out the *Pocket Oxford Dictionary*.

"You better put your name in that," he said, handing it over.

I nodded and began to retreat with the small red dictionary clutched in my hand.

"Congratulations!" he called after me.

I didn't look at my prize until I was back in the Volvo and we were headed to the liquor store to meet our bootlegger. Ignoring the questions from Aldous, I dug around in my shapeless purse, which contained gum wrappers, packages of Player's Light, eyeliner and lip gloss, and a complete absence of school books, until I found a ballpoint pen.

I scribbled my name on the blank page at the front.

Susan Juby

I stared at the signature for a good long while. It looked wrong. I should have waited until the car had stopped. My name looked like it had been scribbled by a five-year-old who'd recently suffered a devastating stroke.

But still.

Fourteen hours later, I woke up in a completely different car. A Trans Am that an older guy had driven into a ditch and left there with me and another girl still inside. My friend and I had decided to spend the night in the car because we'd told our parents that we were staying at each other's houses and the boy who'd been driving said his parents would "have a shit" if they caught two girls in his house.

It was April and the night had been cold and miserable. We were half-frozen and I was still drunk. I looked around to discover that I couldn't find my purse and had lost one of my shoes. There was blood all over my pink jean jacket.

All at once I remembered the little dictionary and began to panic when I couldn't find it. Then I realized that I was hanging on to it.

I didn't write another word of fiction again until I was twenty-seven. That little dictionary still sits on my desk today.

6

The Last Ride

BEFORE I WAS EVER ADDICTED to alcohol I was addicted to horses. The minute I first laid eyes on a horse, I was lost. There was no creature so magnificent, noble, or beautiful as a horse. Giraffes and moose were close, but they weren't as shiny and wouldn't let you ride them. I drew horses on every flat surface and even created a cartoon horse character named Foster Grain. He was a fat little creature who always wore sunglasses. His plot lines were dull, but he had spots on his ass, which more than made up for it.

I learned to make horse noises with my mouth, including the sound of a horse galloping, and I spent an inordinate amount of time going around on hands and knees pretending I was a horse. None of this is unusual. Children have been doing these things probably since the first cave youth saw a Dinohippus. The only thing that was unusual about it is that I continued wearing out the knees in my pants until well past the age when such behaviour could be considered normal.

Finally, when I was around ten and was pretty sure I'd die if I didn't get my own horse, my mother and stepfather said I could take my savings and use the money to buy a horse. I had ridden only a few times and, other than the many books I'd read, had no real knowledge of horses. A family down the road heard that there was a sucker on the lookout and they offered to sell me their horse for eight hundred dollars. The horse in question was an elderly gelding called Echo's Little Wonder. He was supposed to be an Appaloosa, but I think his registration papers may have been fake. He was white with fleabite-looking speckles, stood nearly seventeen hands high and looked like a cross between a fridge and a rhino. With his massive Roman nose, all that was missing was the horn and the freezer compartment. He had a habit of lowering his head and fixing me with a baleful look. I loved Echo and was terrified of him in equal measures.

I kept him at a small farm a few miles away from our place. Each day I would walk an hour there and an hour back to see him. Each day he did his best to scare me to death. Horses are big and Echo was huge. As I spent more time with him, I gained an appreciation for the hundreds of ways one can get hurt around horses, including getting kicked, bitten, squished, and smashed or bucked off. Echo did all of the above to me. Once in a while, for variety, he'd place a plate-sized hoof on my foot and grind it into the earth.

I had only a bridle, and when I first got on him I felt momentarily on top of the world or at least on top of a mountain. I was riding! I was riding!

Then Echo lowered his head and gave a combination shiver/ shrug that landed me on the ground.

I wasn't riding.

I finally figured out how to stay onboard for upwards of ten minutes or longer at a time and we began to venture out of his field and around the neighbourhood. Echo dumped me in mud puddles, creeks, and ditches and onto nearly any other surface you can think of. But he was a gentleman and usually waited for me to get up and brush myself off (or staunch the bleeding) and get back on. This was in the days before many people wore helmets, and there were several occasions when I hit my head hard enough that I couldn't remember my name for several minutes. I blame my inability to do even basic math on some of the brain damage I got from those early concussions. A better name for him would have been Echo's Little Concussion.

As time went on, Echo and I would head out in the morning and come back when the sun fell. We crossed rivers and swam into lakes. We explored every trail and every road. Owning a horse was like having a best friend, confessor, and car all wrapped into one slightly unpredictable package.

After trail riding for a year or two, I got a saddle and started taking riding lessons. My mother had been supportive of my riding before this. She had horses when she was growing up, and she was in favour of anything that kept me busy and out of trouble. She paid for all my riding expenses, including the lessons and shows that I started later. Echo's Little Wonder was not a show horse. He was old. He was huge. He had a rotten attitude and we won nothing.

Echo was finally retired, and my mother bought me a fancier horse, a little mare called Honey. I switched from western to English and then discovered dressage and got more and more into showing. I rode (or at least I was supposed to ride) every day in the summer, and my mother and I drove all over the northern interior going to horse shows.

My focus changed. I started to think about riding in terms of winning and money. Who had the most expensive horse? Who won the most competitions? My mother made serious sacrifices in time and money to pay for my riding. When I was competing, I don't remember her ever buying herself new clothes even though she worked full time. In return, I was expected to be disciplined and take my riding seriously. The problem, of course, was that I had developed other interests. I liked boys and parties. Riding was getting in the way of all that. It was also interfering with my drinking. I still loved horses and I enjoyed doing well at shows, but I liked getting wasted even more.

Near the end of my high school years, a high-level dressage teacher came to Smithers to give a clinic. Somehow, Honey and I caught her eye, and when the clinic was over she asked if I wanted to come and train with her at her barn when I was finished high school. She lived in another country, and the offer forced me to make a decision. Was riding and working with horses what I wanted to do with my life?

After giving it some thought, I decided I wasn't ready to make the commitment. That was the beginning of the end of my riding career. Riding slipped down the list of my priorities until my mother had to nag incessantly to get me to spend any time with my horse at all.

The last show I went to was held at the Smithers Fair Grounds. I had, as usual, entered every possible class. After a successful first day, I made a plan to meet my non-riding friends, Brenda, Charmagne, and Nan, at the midway so we could go on the rides that evening. My mother warned me that I had to be home early in order to be ready to compete the next day. As soon as I had a few drinks with my friends, I forgot all about going home and all about my horse.

It was well past my curfew when my mother arrived at the fair to take me home. I refused to go with her. She lost her cool. She began dragging me through the fairgrounds amid all the strobing lights and jangling music and the sickly scents of dust and vomit and cotton candy. Drunk as I was, I still remember people watching us pass, her leading me by the neck and the arm like a reluctant steer and me resisting all the way.

When we got home, my mother, nearly crying with rage and frustration, informed me that if I couldn't abide by the rules of the house, I was free to leave. Gathering up my wasted dignity and my new down-filled duvet, I walked out of the house and made my way up to the highway, where I stood, wrapped in my quilt, waiting to meet my non-living-at-home/non-horseback-riding destiny.

It was only when the old motorhome screeched to a halt in front of me that I remembered serial killers and their fondness for young, female hitchhikers. They probably especially liked girls wearing quilts in which their bodies could be conveniently wrapped later. I got in anyway. The RV was being driven by two French guys in their late twenties. They were from a small town in Quebec. The first thing they showed me was their prize yogurt container full of pot. We smoked up, which did nothing for my already tenuous emotional well-being. As luck would have it, they were headed for the fair. When they unloaded me and my duvet, I wandered around to discover that my friends had left. I'd run away from home with only a down-filled quilt for nothing.

I ended up at a house party some time later and spent the rest of the night in a blackout. I woke up in a strange room, beside a strange guy, and was instantly filled with the sickening realization that I was homeless. Worse, I'd missed my first class at the horse show. Who was looking after my horse?

I got someone to drive me home and when I walked into the house I was met by my grim-faced family. My mom had gone and picked up Honey from the show grounds. After a horrible conversation during which I promised to behave, I was allowed to come home. But that was the end of my riding career. Not long after, Honey was sold. The horse and the sport that had made life worth living for so long were gone. In truth, I barely noticed.

7

Playing Well with Others

AGAINST ALL ODDS, or maybe because the teachers in middle school wanted nothing more than to get rid of their foul-mouthed charge, I was moved to the high school with the rest of my class. This was when my life started to get very bad. From the outside, I probably looked like just another hormonally challenged and socially confused kid. On the inside, I felt like an ice climber who'd forgotten her crampons. If I had to guess, I'd say the cause of the chaos was eighty percent substance abuse and twenty percent adolescence, though everyone around me continued to attribute all my problems to my age and the fact that I was a ninth grader.

As far as I was concerned, the problem was my personal relationships. Like Henry in *Barfly*, I didn't hate people, but I seemed to feel better when they weren't around. I'd let go of my gentle and accepting best friend Giselle in order to hang out with people who partied, but my new friendships weren't solid, as I found out when I made the mistake of briefly dating, then breaking up with, a boy.

He was one of the wild ones. As I got to know him better, I would more likely have described him as one of the dumb ones. Hank was decent looking, even attractive, with olive skin and a wide toothy grin. The problem was that he insisted on talking. He was under the impression that just because he thought something, he should say it out loud. His particular specialty was stating the obvious. Later it was plotting the least romantic ways conceivable to relieve me of my virginity.

I agreed to "go out" with Hank one night when a few of us were drinking in a baseball dugout near town. I was splitting my time between my popular friends and the wild ones. That particular night, the two groups mingled. I was very drunk, and the powerful ringing in my ears made it impossible to understand anything Hank said to me. I didn't even realize what I'd done until I got a call from Darcy the next morning.

"So, you and Hank, eh?" she said.

I had recently finished dry-retching as quietly as possible so my family wouldn't hear and was attempting to keep a sip of flat ginger ale down. As usual, I was afflicted with soul-destroying remorse. I'd been in a blackout for most of the night before, so I wasn't exactly sure what I was sorry for. All I knew was that I was very, very sorry.

"Hank?" I said.

"Don't you remember? You guys got together? You were sitting on his knee the whole night. It was so cute."

"Hank?" I said. I was having trouble remembering his face. I'd been in grade nine for only a couple of weeks, and everyone and everything was a still blur. This wasn't helped by the fact that I'd recently started smoking extra pot in an attempt to become more easygoing. As noted previously, pot had the exact opposite effect on me that it seemed to have on everyone else. It made me paranoid and, when mixed with alcohol, violent. In other words, I was more of an aspirational pothead.

"Ha. Ha. Very funny. I wish I was going out with an older guy," said Darcy.

"How old is he again?"

"Grade eleven. He's so hot."

All at once the memories began to crash in. Hank, curly haired, possessed of tremendous, if, in my opinion, misguided, personal confidence. *That guy* was my new boyfriend? How could that have happened? I fell back into bed like I'd been punched by a god-sized fist.

The next call came a few minutes later.

"Is this Susan?"

"Yes," I said.

"How's it going?"

"Uh, fine?" I said. It seemed rude to ask who was speaking.

"Right on. Hey, you want to meet up later?"

Vomit lurched into my throat as I realized who was probably on the other end of the line.

"I can't. I've got to … I mean, I'm grounded. Because of last night."

"That sucks," said the caller who was probably Hank.

"Yeah," I said.

"Can you sneak out?" asked Almost Certainly Hank.

"No. My mom is, she's like, tough," I said, improvising.

"Well, that fucking sucks," said Definitely Hank.

"Well, I have to go now. I'm not supposed to use the phone."

"What if your house goes on fire?"

"There are exceptions," I said.

"See you at school Monday," he said and hung up. His words felt like a threat.

Sure enough, he was waiting for me outside in the smoking area Monday morning. He didn't smoke, but he spent a lot of time out there anyway. It was where all the people who liked to party hung out. As soon as he saw me, he strode over and slung an arm around my neck, like I was an old army buddy he'd once saved from enemy fire. Very possessive, that arm.

"Hey," he said.

The hangover from Friday night when I'd apparently enlisted with Hank's unit had been epic, but it was nothing compared to the swamp of excess stomach acids and random poisons now being churned out by my knotted digestive system.

All the smoking area people eyed us approvingly and I tried not to shrink away from Hank. Instead, I offered him a weak smile.

"Hey."

That should have been it. No one said much in the smoking area, other than "Got a smoke?" and "Fuck off" or "She's such a bitch." But Hank, as a non-smoker, wasn't busy smoking so he was free to hold forth on a variety of subjects, such as how many pull-ups he could do and how fast he could run.

His arm prevented me from smoking comfortably. His conversation prevented me from breathing properly. I could nearly feel the situation turning into an uncontrolled asthma attack.

"You want to skip next period?" he whispered intimately, his hint of moustache tickling my ear.

I cranked my head to the side to avoid it.

"No!" I blurted. Then tried to soften it. "I've got class."

"Fuck class. I want to spend time with you."

For some reason, the severity of my reaction to him was all out of proportion to anything he'd said or done. Sure, he was dumb. But so was I. So was almost everyone I knew. We were in a dumb phase of life. The problem was that Hank, like many of the other guys I ever hooked up with when I was drinking, revolted me when

I was sober. I had no respect for anyone whose self-esteem was so crappy that they could be interested in me.

In the harsh light of the smoking area, I couldn't bear to look at Hank. If he didn't get his arm off me soon, I was going to chew off my own arm at the shoulder.

"I've got a test," I told him. It could have been true. A lot of people had them. Or so I'd heard.

"Sucks ass."

"Okay, bye!" I slipped out from under the encircling arm and threw my cigarette on the concrete.

"Hey!" he said. It was his second favourite word, after "sucks."

I looked at him, trying to control my breathing.

"Aren't you going to give me a kiss?" he asked, loud enough so everyone could hear.

I stared at him, appalled at the idea. That's when he kissed me. His mouth was so wet that it felt like he had licked me.

Everyone cheered. Quite the romantic moment in the smoking area.

It took me until lunch to get the taste out of my mouth.

"I swear I will never drink again," I muttered to myself during the four visits I made to the girls' washroom to make disgusted faces at myself in the mirror and wipe off and reapply my lipstick. "I swear, God, I will never drink again if you will just make Hank go away."

God wasn't listening and Hank didn't go away. He spent the hours we were apart planning elaborate strategies to "get me alone," according to reports from my delighted friends. He was eager for us to "do it."

I had no idea why people were so overjoyed at the prospect. Probably because some of the wild girls had nasty boyfriends who expected them to do it and they wanted everyone to take part in the misery.

At lunch I hid, but when I saw the wild ones between third and fourth periods, they gave me updates on Hank's plans.

"He's going to ask you to go to Steve's house."

"Actually Steve's garage," corrected another.

"So you guys can be alone."

"To do it."

My stomach heaved at the thought of being alone with the wet-mouthed, monosyllabic boy.

I fled home before last period, telling my teacher I was sick. When the phone rang that afternoon and then again approximately every twenty minutes, I didn't answer it. When my mother got home (she was the only other person who answered the phone in our house), I told her too that I was too sick to speak to anyone.

Huddled in my bed, my mind spun with ways to get rid of Hank. I composed numerous letters.

"Dear Hank, I have decided I am too young to date."

or

"Dear Hank, I'm not ready for a relationship. Also, you should know that I was in a blackout when I agreed to go out with you."

or

"Dear Hank, my mother says I can't see you any more because there's a chance you might be bad news. Sorry."

or

"Dear Hank, we probably shouldn't go out because I'm bad news."

or

"Dear Hank, you make me want to throw up so I don't think we should see each other any more."

And so on, ad infinitum.

With the greatest reluctance in the world, I dragged myself off to school the next morning. Unlike my usual outfit of skin-tight painter pants and T-shirt, I cloaked myself in oversized sweatpants and one of my mother's less attractive gardening sweaters. I hoped the vast clothing would make me less irresistible. Unfortunately, Hank apparently would have found a stuffed footstool erotic.

He bounded over the second I sidled into the smoking area, which I did only because I didn't think I could survive the morning without a smoke.

"Hey!" he nearly bellowed. And I was certain he was going to go for another kiss. So I took a step back and said, somewhat less than diplomatically, "I don't want to go out with you."

"WHAAAA?" said Hank, stopping mid-leap like a startled water buffalo.

"Sorry," I said, my gaze skittering from side to side, taking in the fascinated smoking area onlookers.

It took Hank a minute or two to realize what was happening, but once he did, he also grasped that he'd just been dumped in front of a crowd and that was not cool. Not cool at all.

"Why?" he said, his chin jutting into my airspace.

My hands shook as I lit my cigarette. "I just can't go out with you," I said, my voice trembling a little to go with the fluttery hands.

"Who do you think you are?" demanded Hank.

"Who do you think *you* are?" I retorted. I was tired of being scared of Hank, and my fear was starting to harden into anger.

"You get out of here," he said, gesturing around the butt-strewn patch of concrete that constituted the smoking area. "This is my territory."

"Why? Did you piss on it?"

I'm not sure whether Hank was familiar with the animal behaviour concept to which I was alluding. But he knew an insult when he heard one.

"Bitch," he said. "Whore."

"Asshole," I muttered. "Prick."

Then, with weak legs, I removed myself from the scene, leaving mouths hanging open all over the butt patch.

It soon became clear that I'd made a serious strategic error by crossing Hank so publicly. I hadn't noticed before, but quite a few of the wild ones were, at heart, conservative. Many of the girls let the boys take the lead in all things but shoplifting. In a mixed group, the majority of the jokes were told by boys, even though the girls were funnier and more interesting. Some of the toughest, sassiest, and most violent girls acted like docile little waifs around their boyfriends. I might have had terrifically low self-esteem and been afraid of boys, but I didn't think they were worthy of unquestioned respect.

And I'd apparently let that particular cat out of the bag in a flagrant display of ill temper.

It turned out the cure for uppity, a.k.a. conceited, girls who weren't grateful for a perfectly good (if dim-witted) boy was a good beat down, to be administered by the other girls.

Around this time a couple of the wildest girls were testing the limits of their power by getting into harder drugs and hanging out with ever-dodgier people. Darcy and Tara, one of the ringleaders of the wild ones, had apparently started doing a lot of acid and mushrooms, which we called "shrooms" because we were cool like that. They were also rumoured to be hanging out with much older guys, who in turn hung around second-string bikers. Tara and Darcy hadn't just jumped the tracks. They'd launched themselves into outer space. God only knows what was going on in their lives that they got so out of control so quickly, but by the second week of high school, they'd started terrorizing people at random. One day the smallest girl in the school, a tiny person with a hat-like head of hair, had the temerity to look at them. They followed her outside at lunch and slapped her around. Needless to say, it wasn't much of a contest and the girl was left scratched and weeping.

When her equally petite mom came to get her, Darcy and Tara went after her, too. It was surreal to see a mother scurrying away from ninth graders, at once unsettling and exciting. All the rules of the universe had been upended. Here was proof that chaos reigned in high school.

During Darcy and Tara's first episodes of indiscriminate violence I maintained a level of detachment, partly due to shell shock at finding myself in high school and partly because I was focused on getting rid of Hank. My detachment lasted exactly until I dumped Hank and became Darcy and Tara's next target.

It was as though I'd never met either of them before, even though we'd been drinking and hanging out together for years.

"Tara's looking for you. She says she's going to kick your ass," reported a girl named Pam, whose locker was next to mine.

I had been about to head to the smoking area.

"Why?" I blurted. "What did I do?"

"Her and Darcy say it wasn't cool what you did to Hank," said Pam, shaking her head sadly. Pam was the official bearer of bad news.

A few of the other girls who'd gathered around us nodded in agreement with the verdict.

"Not cool. Not cool at all," they said.

And that was it. I'd gone from marginally acceptable to full-scale pariah in less than two hours. Damn that Hank.

The only reason Tara and Darcy hadn't been kicked out of school yet is that they hadn't been caught. They didn't go to classes. They just showed up, wasted, at breaks and beat the crap out of anyone who got in their way. And now they were after me. No one was going to save me or stick up for me. I knew that instinctively. It was like I'd just been targeted by Stalin's secret police: everyone was paranoid that if they got in the way, they'd be next. Charmagne, Brenda, and Nan and every other friend and acquaintance I had melted away.

I was already an abnormally fearful person. Being out in public while sober was hard. Being at school, surrounded by my peers, many of whom I found terrifying, was worse. I couldn't drink at school because I couldn't hide it like some people could, and I wasn't ready to quit or do something to get kicked out permanently (although the odd suspension was fine). Now, all my unnamed anxiety was taking on a face and an identity. I had something to be scared of and I was up to the job.

After Pam delivered the news, I didn't know what to do. I couldn't hide in a washroom. Tara and Darcy were big on washrooms. Instead I went out a side door to smoke in relative safety. I couldn't control my breathing. The feeling of being in a waking nightmare was as bad as any hangover I'd yet experienced.

I congratulated myself on surviving the break and was just about to slip through the side door and head to class when Tara materialized from around the corner.

"Where do you think you're going?" she asked.

"Nowhere," I said.

The funny thing was that I felt almost no surprise that this girl had gone from acquaintance to attacker in such a short time and without any real discussion. Since I'd started drinking, and maybe even before, I'd begun to feel that human relations teetered on the verge of violence all the time. This experience only confirmed it. Getting wasted together didn't constitute undying loyalty.

I can't remember what else Tara and Darcy said. What I do remember is that when Tara reached out to slap me, I tried to block her hand, but she was too fast. It was like getting stung by a bionic wasp. Sugar Ray Leonard on PCP.

Slap! My head snapped back.

Slap! My head snapped to the side.

Ring! The bell signalled the end of the break, and when I opened my eyes I saw that we were surrounded by people.

I held a hand to my stinging face in amazement.

"That's a taste of what you're going to get at lunch," said Tara.

Then she and Darcy melted away before some teacher could come along and officially suspend them.

A taste. Dear god, what would a whole meal be like?

I didn't know what to do.

If I'd been different, if I'd thought adults could help or would want to, maybe I'd have tried to talk to one. If I'd been even a little bit outraged at this sudden, terrifying turn of events, maybe I'd have tried to do something other than allow the nightmare to unfold in slow motion. But some part of me felt like I deserved it. My drinking had already chipped away at my self-esteem enough that I felt like a beating was even overdue. This is what happened to girls who drank too much. This is what happened to people who were bad news. I wandered from class to class like a shell-shocked prisoner on a forced march until lunch.

When the bell rang, I stayed in my seat until everyone else had gone, including the two or three wild ones who were also in Social Studies with me.

"Let's go," said the teacher. "I've got to close up the room."

"I just …" I said. I just what? I'm just afraid to leave? I couldn't tell him that.

Instead I stood and gathered my books and forced myself to walk out into the hallway. They surrounded me right away. At least five or six of them. The teacher left the classroom and locked it. He looked in our direction and then kept going.

Tara was in the middle of the pack, and as soon as the teacher left, she was in my face.

"Darcy is going to take you outside and teach you a lesson," she said.

Her pupils were pinned and I could smell the booze on her breath. I looked over her shoulder to see Darcy, who looked considerably less certain about the situation. She seemed to be in the grip of some desire to please Tara and some need to quench her own confusion and anger. I felt a flicker of sympathy, like I was viewing all of us from above.

In a mass, the little gang of girls edged me toward the nearest door that led outside. They manoeuvred me down the stairs and into a little alcove so we were hidden from view. At the last moment, I balked and tried to stop myself from being shoved outside. I grabbed the door jamb, but Darcy pulled me by the arm and soon the door closed behind us.

I could hear the whispers: fight, fight, fight. Like a chant, or a curse.

The fight itself had an even more pronounced nightmare quality, jerky and surreal, like a poor-quality videotape spliced together with old Scotch Tape.

Darcy and I faced each other. Her face was puffy and slightly yellow. Her eyes were unfocused and there were eyeliner boogers in the corners.

Some bad dialogue was exchanged, along the lines of "Well, what do you have to say for yourself?" and the ever-popular "Who do you think you are?" To which I replied, "Nothing" and "No one."

Then Darcy slapped me across the face. Once, twice.

"Come on," she said, gaining confidence when she realized she was battling a dedicated pacifist. "Hit me."

And that's when the quality of the recollection really deteriorates.

According to the people watching, I grabbed her hair, which was dark and slightly curly, kneed her in the crotch (I do have three brothers), and began methodically smashing her head into the brick wall of the schoolyard. I felt nothing. I heard nothing but the rush of blood in my head. My next memory is of sitting in the principal's office, weeping uncontrollably, even though I was unscathed. Darcy acted more like a hardened con in a Baltimore interrogation room than a ninth grader from Smithers. That part still impresses me. Her eyes were blackened, the side of her face was scratched raw, both her lips were fat. The principal listened to my account, garbled by my persistent sobs. Darcy said only "Fuck you" to me and something similar to the principal. And when it was over, she was kicked out of school indefinitely and I was not.

My total blackout rage dominance in the fight didn't do anything for my social standing. Instead, there was a long period during which almost no one would speak to me. The stigma of having been in a fight, as a winner or a loser, took some time to fade. I was verboten to all but a few gentle souls, who made a point of asking how I was and occasionally joining me as I ate lunch alone beside my locker.

Did this mean that I took a good hard look at my drinking, which had led to this mess? After all, if I hadn't been drunk, I would never have ended up going out with Hank. If Darcy and Tara hadn't been on a big bender, they probably wouldn't have attacked me. If I didn't drink as much as or more than they did, we would never have hung out with each other in the first place. Booze and drugs were the common denominator in all the disasters that had befallen me. But I didn't see it that way.

I was acutely conscious of being shunned and I hated missing all the parties because it wasn't yet safe for me to go to them. My only conversations were with girls who didn't drink, sneak out, smoke pot, dabble in coke, or take mushrooms, which meant that I had no one to do those things with. There was only one cure that I could see, and it was one that my mom actually agreed with.

It was time to take the Susan Juby, Juvenile Delinquent, Show on the road.

8

Wherever You Go

AS A KID I'd spent every summer with much-loved aunts and uncles and grandparents in the Okanagan. My grandparents had a rickety little cabin announced by an old wooden sign as Harry's Hideaway. The cabin had a screened-in porch and a set of steep, wobbly rock stairs that led down to a pebbled beach, and there was a silvered old wharf that extended into Shuswap Lake.

I loved the Okanagan in the summer and was completely fascinated by my uncles. They were younger than my mother. They all wore beards and were married to good-looking women who, to my inexperienced eye, were shockingly into nudity. This last quality was passed along to my cousins, who seemed rarely to wear much more than socks. In our family, we barely even got naked while alone in the shower. It was as though the entire family's inhibitions skipped a generation and all landed on me. I'm not saying my aunts and uncles and cousins were nudists, exactly. It was more that they occasionally skinny-dipped, and when they got changed into their bathing suits they didn't padlock the door, put a chair against the knob, and hang three blankets in the window like I did. To me, that kind of relaxed approach was pretty much the same thing as being a full-on exhibitionist.

There was a lot of drinking at the cabin, but it was Okanagan *summer drinking*, which seemed to be a more genteel, good-natured sort of drinking than the kind that took place during northern B.C. winters.

My grandparents were old-fashioned imbibers. Slow and steady could have been the motto for their alcohol consumption. They travelled a lot in their later years, and in every photo I've ever seen of them in every foreign locale, they have highball glasses clutched in their hands. So do all their friends. From my grandparents I learned that five o'clock cocktails were the best and most important part of the day. Drinking had meaning. It had purpose as well as ritual and a certain dignity.

When things went bad for me in Smithers, I decided that I needed to move to Salmon Arm, the town where all of my uncles resided when they weren't visiting the cabin, which was farther around the lake. I figured that a change of scenery would give me a fresh start. Plus, I was attracted to the classy drinking they practised there. My aunts and uncles, all kind-hearted, generous, and deeply unprepared for what they were getting into, said they'd love to put me up. (At least that's how I remember it. It's possible they had their arms twisted by my mother, who was probably running out of ideas about what to do with me.)

After I spent the summer at the cabin, I moved in with my first set of relatives, my uncle and his wife, for the school year. My aunt and uncle had five kids of their own already and lived in a pair of domes onto which my uncle, a contractor, had built a rambling, marvellous house. The whole place functioned like a pinball machine named Chaos.

My aunt and uncle probably thought that one more kid wouldn't make much difference. Turns out they were wrong because I wasn't like their other kids. For one thing, I was optional. For another, I was about to enter my junior drinky-pants "complete meltdown" phase.

About thirty seconds after I arrived in Salmon Arm and entered my new school, I wore out my welcome with my classmates. I once again briefly dated, then for no good reason broke up with, a somewhat popular boy, thereby alienating all of his friends. I took one of my hitherto clean-living younger cousins out and got her drunk on some booze I'd stolen from her parents. I don't remember this, but another of my cousins told me that once I forgot my makeup on the bus and refused to go to school again until it was replaced and I could get my mask on before being seen in public.

Soon my new school and living situation were as uncomfortable as or worse than the ones I'd left behind. The cousin I'd gotten drunk, who was a year younger than me, found me so hard to live with that she started hoarding her allowance to save up enough money to take out a "hit" on me. My aunt and uncle woke to find me belly-crawling like a soldier across their bedroom floor at one o'clock in the morning, drunk and in hot pursuit of my uncle's cigarettes. My plan was to secure some smokes and then round up a few cousins to go cross-country skiing.

Shortly afterward, I went to live with my second set of relatives. This uncle was my mother's youngest brother. He and I had always been simpatico. He was my godfather and we had the same world view. We could talk for hours about our philosophies of life and what was wrong with almost everyone else.

My godfather had struggled with substance abuse himself, until my aunt gave him an ultimatum. He could have her or alcohol and drugs. He very wisely chose her. I didn't really remember him as a drinker and carouser, but family legend had it that he used to travel with the equivalent of a small but well-stocked pharmacy in his luggage. When I went to live with them, he'd been clean and sober for years. Obviously, if anyone could handle me and my issues, it would be him.

Sadly, I was in such a state by the time I moved in that I'd have challenged a crack team from an elite treatment centre. Soon after I moved into town to live with my unsuspecting young aunt and uncle, I had what, in retrospect, was probably some sort of private nervous breakdown. I became profoundly irrational and depressed. I remember only a few random details from those months, but the ones I do remember are strange and vivid. I would eat only Ichiban noodles (original flavour) for breakfast, lunch, and dinner and I insisted on eating them alone in my room. I had a large Billy Idol poster tacked on the wall in my bedroom and I would stare at it for hours, as though at some point Billy would stop sneering and start telling me how to get through high school. That's what I was doing, alone in my room, hour after hour.

Like pretty much everyone else, my aunt and uncle thought I was going through a teen phase of some sort, only a bit worse than average. In a way they were right. Their own kids were young and they had no experience with teenagers. Lots of teens do lock themselves in their rooms when they aren't at school. Some may even have a fetish for instant noodles. We have an eccentric family, so probably from the outside, I just seemed mildly temperamental. On the inside, I was in a strange sort of fugue state. Maybe it was brought on from the previous year's fights and drinking and problems at school, or maybe I depended more on the particular structure of my family than I'd thought to keep me together. The realization that I was just as much a disaster in the Okanagan as I had been in the northern interior was a terrible blow. Probably it was a combination of all of those things that caused my little crack-up. Whatever it was, it felt like a continuation and amplification of my previous unhappy state. I was not well in my brain, but as is so often the case with head problems, I was too close to it to realize what was going on.

The only social interaction I got was when I went out on Friday or Saturday night with a boy named Ben. He was also from Smithers and had moved to Salmon Arm at the same time. He was a couple of years older, and I'm not sure why he hung around with me. I guess he was finding the new town lonely, too, although I'm sure he was nowhere near as unpopular as I was.

He would pick me up in his parents' old Subaru and we'd drive aimlessly around town. He would smoke joint after joint, and I'd consume one or more of the bottles of homemade wine that his parents made and stored in their basement. He'd get high and I'd get alcohol poisoning, the symptoms of which included mild blindness and a whole lot of oblivion. I often stayed overnight at his house.

Ben and I never hooked up romantically. Neither of us had any interest. I existed in a fog of misery and disconnection and just wanted someone to get obliterated with. I assume it was the same for him. It was the most functional relationship I'd had with a boy up to that point.

After a few weeks of my highly restrictive and nutrient-free diet and my habit of drinking myself into a rot-gut red-wine stupor once a week, I started to display the early symptoms of scurvy. My gums, never the best thanks to iffy oral hygiene and long-term braces, as well as drinking and smoking, began to bleed freely and often at the slightest provocation, such as when I opened my mouth, which luckily, I did only to eat instant noodles and drink wine. Naturally, I decided that the only thing that could save me from complete mental disintegration and dental disaster was the love of a good dog.

I knew it was risky to introduce a pet into my packed social schedule of one blacked-out evening per week with a boy who was likely also in the grips of a devastating depression. But I became obsessed with the heartwarming image of a dog, probably some sort of collie, waiting for me at the limits of the school property. We would walk home together, and all the other kids at school would see how devoted that dog was and realize they were missing out on a good thing by not hanging around with or even talking to me. My cousin, who went to the same school and was still trying to hire someone to beat me up, would also realize that I had many excellent qualities, even though they weren't immediately apparent. A dog was definitely the answer to all my problems!

I got so wrapped up in my fantasies of dog companionship that the lines between imagination and reality blurred. I wanted a dog so bad it felt almost like I already *had* one. I was that committed. They say that serious drinkers and druggers stop growing emotionally at the age they start using. This couldn't be true because I didn't start drinking when I was six, but that's exactly where I seemed to have stopped maturing.

I was devastated when my godfather informed me that I could not get a dog while I was living with them. For some reason my aunt and uncle seemed to think that a girl who wouldn't come out of her room, who stared for hours at a poster of Billy Idol, and who refused to eat anything other than instant noodles was not ready for the sort of serious responsibility dog ownership entails. I cried for days. At least it *felt* like days.

"But it's not fair!" I screeched.

My uncle said, not unkindly, "Life's not fair. You know that, right?"

The impact of his statement threw me back in my seat.

Life was not fair. Not fair!?

What the high holy hell kind of a thing was that to say to a person?

It remains one of the single worst pieces of news I ever got.

I was so upset that my aunt and uncle became alarmed, and when I changed tack and asked for a rabbit, they caved.

This was a mistake.

As anyone who has ever known a rabbit can attest, they are not noted for their affectionate natures. Well, maybe some are, but only when great piles and heaps of attention are lavished on them by very special owners. I was not a special owner. I was a chronically immature young alcoholic in the midst of some indeterminate personal breakdown.

At the pet store I chose the most exotic-looking bunny, because looks are important. Not the looks of one's gums, necessarily, but the looks of one's accessories, pets, and posters. I got a jet-black mini-lop-eared rabbit that, after long consideration, I named Valotte, after Julian Lennon's first album. I thought my rabbit's name would mark me as a serious music lover, touched by the greatness of the son of a former Beatle. No one got the reference because Julian never really took off, so I changed the bunny's name to Strummer, after The Clash's Joe Strummer.

Strummer's main talent turned out to be crouching in a baleful black ball and producing thousands upon thousands of small round poops. He did not enjoy snuggling and struggled and scratched me when I attempted to hold him. If I persisted for too long in my attempts to "gentle" him, he pooped on me and sometimes peed.

He did nothing to help my floundering self-esteem and in fact may have made it worse. It turned out that being the owner of an unfriendly rabbit was not the social stimulant I'd imagined. There was no way to even show my classmates that at least one creature liked me because (a) I was too old for show and tell, (b) Strummer wouldn't allow me to hold him long enough to get him to school, and (c) I would have looked like a complete ass trying to lug his enormous cage down the hill to the school building.

A month or so after getting the rabbit that was supposed to change my life, I decided to move again, this time out of my aunt and uncle's place and in with my grandmother. Reluctantly, I brought Strummer with me.

What I really wanted was to go home to Smithers. I realized that the problems I had at home weren't about the town, where I was sure I still had friends, even if they'd kept a low profile during my time as school pariah. The problem was Salmon Arm, which had sold me a bill of goods about how fun it was. That classy summer drinking? Total bullshit. I didn't get one bit better at drinking. I repeatedly asked my mother if I could come home and she said no. She said I had to stick out the school year.

Her firmness on the subject had one good effect. When I finally got to go home to Smithers in June, I was, for the first time ever, grateful to be there. I put the increasingly sex-crazed Strummer into our chicken coop, where he spent his time attempting to hump any hen who came near him. I was ready for another fresh start now that I had my hometown in perspective. Still, I told anyone who asked that I had a fantastic time in Salmon Arm. I displayed pictures of all my new friends, most of whom I'd barely known. I made it sound like I was doing the town of Smithers a favour by returning.

A month later, after a few more drinking episodes, I was again making plans to get the hell out. The problem was obviously the small-town environment. What I needed was a major city in order to really shine.

9

Quit All This?

PEOPLE SOMETIMES ASK if anyone ever said anything to me about my drinking, and the truth is that no one did. Well, almost no one. Once a bouncer at the local cabaret watched as I picked myself up after my legs went out from under me a fourth or fifth time as I tried to leave the dance floor. This happened quite a bit and helped to explain why I was usually covered with bruises.

"Why do you always get so drunk?" he asked, genuinely puzzled.

His words rattled around in my head for a long time afterward. Why indeed? In truth, I didn't know how to drink any other way. I genuinely couldn't see the point of moderate drinking. The whole goal of drinking was to get wasted. Really wasted. Drinking and blacking out gave me a much-needed holiday from myself. And sometimes, it was extremely fun. In my last years of high school, I had many friends and we had excellent adventures when we were drinking. From the outside, it probably looked like I was having a great time. But inside I felt the same as I had in elementary school when I was the target of any kid with a lunch box–cudgel.

Right from the start, I knew I had a drinking problem. But I thought of it as my cultural and environmental legacy as much as part of my genetic makeup. Most of the people I knew drank. Old people, young people. Really young people. Some people drank even more than I did, although most didn't attract as much negative attention as I did.

In Smithers in the 1980s it was more unusual not to drink than it was to be a serious drinker. At least, that's how I remember it. When someone couldn't handle their drink or drugs, we said they were "screwed up" or "assholes." Or possibly "sluts" or "losers." We didn't think they were drunks or addicts. The only people who were officially drunks were the semi-homeless people (all three of them) who drank at the picnic tables on the stretch of grass in between the government building and the library and the older guys glued to bar stools seven nights a week from five until closing and the middle-aged ladies who showed up at the liquor store the minute it opened. They were drunks. The rest of us, especially those who were young, were "partiers."

That said, I sensed that there was something different about the way I drank and the way my friends did. Most of us got loaded regularly, some of us blacked out often. The difference between me and the others was my mysterious super-ability to piss people off. People noticed me when I was drunk. Many observers thought I was a little mentally unbalanced. I had an uncanny knack for saying and doing exactly the wrong thing at the wrong time. If someone had just lost a parent in an accident, I was likely to make a speech about how people needed to brush off adversity and be independent. If someone had a physical disability, I would bring it up in a way that was just indirect and inappropriate enough to make everyone uncomfortable. I'd make jokes about prison rape to people whose boyfriends were in jail. I was a complete asshole, but an inadvertent one. My friends used to issue cautions to me before we went out, the way you'd warn a kid not to touch anything before heading into a store. "Now Susan," Charmagne would say, "I hope you're going to have a good night tonight and not say anything to Jill about how her uncle was just charged with molesting her." Having a good night meant not getting into a fist fight or antagonizing an entire team's worth of rugby players by casting aspersions on the size of their penises. Having a good night meant not taking off my clothes at the first opportunity or falling down into random bodies of water. When I managed to avoid these things and the myriad other hazards that litter the heavy drinker's landscape, my friends would be amazed. "Wow! You were really good last night!"

I tried to be good when drinking. I really did. I even wrote notes to remind myself. The notes said things like "Don't call [ex-boyfriend/someone else's boyfriend] at 4:00 in the morning." "Don't tell so-and-so that her loser boyfriend is cheating on her and ask her why she didn't see it coming." "Don't hit anyone."

I would pay close attention to how I processed the first couple of drinks. Usually, I was in such a state of roiling anticipation that I started out shaky and lightheaded. The first drink settled me down. The second one lightened my mood. When I went to the bathroom, usually after the second drink, I'd sit on the toilet and do a quick self-check, a sort of alcoholic insight meditation.

"How are you doing?" I'd ask myself. "You upset about anything? Nervous?" I was extra-vigilant for signs of excessive paranoia or unreasoning anger.

This little check-in rarely helped. I'd start out cautious and aware of all the many things I wasn't supposed to do. I would stick by my plan to drink nothing harder than beer or ciders. I wouldn't mix drinks and I'd leave the hard stuff, including the cocaine, strictly alone. But by drink four I had no defences. I did cocaine so I could drink more. I took speed so I could drink more. But drugs were never the main event for me—booze was.

Some nights veered with no warning from a high-spirited silliness into a nightmare. Other nights things stayed light. Sometimes things started screwy and just got worse. I had many, many good nights while drinking. I had even more nightmarish ones, especially as time went on.

One thing I almost never did was try to quit drinking after I'd started. On a couple of occasions I was forced to, but stopping midstream was like crashing face-first into a jagged rock. I stopped drinking when I passed out or when it was incredibly late and we'd finally run out of booze.

Occasionally I would moderate if I didn't think there would be enough alcohol to get drunk, but that was rarely the case at parties in my crowd. I only drank with other people, which was another thing that told me I still had things somewhat under control. But in truth, getting loaded was about getting out of myself. The last thing on earth I wanted was to spend more time alone with myself and my thoughts. Beneath it all, I was catastrophically lonely, even when from outside I looked fine (at least when I wasn't drunk).

In addition to the notes, I prepared for other mishaps by bringing a toothbrush and toothpaste everywhere I went (as noted, I was an inveterate vomiter). Once an older woman whom I used to see at parties told me that one day I'd "learn how to drink like a grown-up." Bringing a toothbrush to parties was as far as I got along that path.

The other thing that made quitting seem impossible was that I was too young. No one quits using and drinking when they're eighteen or nineteen. At least, no one I knew did. I'd tried lots of times and failed miserably. I knew I could never do it on my own. Almost every time I got drunk (once or twice a week), I woke up sick, wracked with remorse, and vowed to quit. Drinking wasn't worth the pain it caused. I would go around for a day or two in a state of shaky shamefacedness and wallow in abject humiliations, real and imagined. Example: the time I went to my friend's birthday party and pretended to drown in her pool no less than four times in front of her whole family as part of a tragic bid for attention. I was incredibly sorry about that and everything else, and to atone I would never drink again.

But after a day or two, I'd feel better and people would start to forget the ass I'd made of myself on the weekend. Then my irritability and hypersensitivity would surface. The resentments and paranoia that I nurtured like Chia pets would sprout and grow so smothering that it became hard to breathe, much less think. A day or so later, I'd be at a party and have three drinks down before I'd remember that I'd meant to quit. There was no decision-making. I would get drunk with no thought of the consequences. I had a strange blind spot and could not make the connection between the messes I made when drunk and the need to refuse when faced with a drink. There was no power of choice. I knew instinctively that this wasn't something normal people understood.

In grade eleven, I started telling people I was an alcoholic. I did this only when I was drunk. I guess I was practising saying the truth out loud. No one seemed very impressed or even very interested.

What I didn't say is that I couldn't quit on my own. Nor did I mention the long-term plan that was beginning to develop in the back of my mind. I knew there was one way to quit. I'd seen several people in my family do it. My biological father, my adoptive father, and an uncle had all gone into a self-help program and actually stopped drinking. Obviously, that was an extreme measure and one best left to older people and not young, vivacious people like me. But if things ever got really out of hand,

I would try it. When I was thirty or so, engaged to be married to a nice man, and ready to settle into domestic bliss, I'd go to some sort of program.

In the meantime, when the bouncer said, "Why do you always get so drunk?" the only honest answer I could think of was one he wouldn't understand. I felt like everything in my life—my friends, lifestyle, location, and age—pointed me in one direction. I always got so drunk because I had to.

10

The Crinoline As Life Preserver

GRADE ELEVEN WAS a turning point for me and for a lot of people I knew. Would I, like many of my friends had done, simply fade out of school? In my crowd, there was never any big announcement about quitting. We just simply … stopped … going. Dropping out was a process that started in grade eight and, for many, finished in grade eleven.

On the other side of the academic scene was the one group in our school who were absolutely certain to graduate. They were the kids who took a program called Directed Studies, developed and run by Mr. Lee. Directed Studies was designed to allow the gifted students to explore their many and varied talents; it enabled the smartest kids in the school to mingle with other similarly gifted young people (as though they didn't already huddle together like the last survivors of some anti-intellectual rebellion). Anyway, in Directed Studies, or DS, as it was known, students got to choose a field of study and develop their own curricula. They went on retreats, presumably to discuss the trials and tribulations of being brilliant: "It's gotten to the stage where particle physics (neuroscience, nanotechnology, etc.) simply isn't enough of a challenge for me any more" or "I am so smart it's actually sort of painful." At the end of every year they gave a public presentation to show the school and larger community what they'd learned. At least, that's what I'd heard. I'd certainly never gone to a

DS presentation or given the program much thought. It was like the chess club, reserved for academic overachievers, the intellectual "haves and have mores," as the second Mr. Bush might have put it. I was too busy murdering brain cells on the weekends with a combination of alcohol and pills and cocaine to be contemplating such a foreign country as Directed Studies.

As previously noted, I was not a member of the academic elite. My friends and I hung out in the smoking area; many of us had boyfriends who drove large trucks and loud cars and hadn't appeared in any graduating class photos. I had permed, feathered hair and a strong preference for black eyeliner and clothing with extra zippers. When I wasn't sleeping during class, I was talking.

In spite of my status as a waste of space in a classroom setting, Mr. Lee was pretty nice to me. As well as Directed Studies, he taught English. Maybe he had a bit more tolerance for me than did the other teachers because we shared an enthusiasm for reading. I read everything on the assigned reading list in the first month of school and, unlike most of my classmates, I actually loved the books chosen. And I liked talking about them in class, even though my comments were usually less than penetrating.

"Can anyone tell me the theme of Orwell's *Nineteen Eighty-Four*?" he'd ask.

I would raise my hand into the deafening silence.

"Yes, Susan?"

"It's about when the whole world becomes like school. It's a drag. You can't get any privacy and stuff. Total fascism, man."

"Hmmm, yes. I see," he'd say, diplomatically.

The difference between Mr. Lee and the rest of the teachers is that he actually called on me when I raised my hand. Few others dared.

Our agreement on the general excellence of books didn't mean I was producing top-notch work or anything. I wasn't scoring straight A's in English, belying my otherwise abysmal performance in school. Any hopes Mr. Lee had that my interest in the class readings would translate into academic success were dashed when I produced mediocre, last-minute papers. But Mr. Lee didn't give up or treat me like the C student I so obviously was. And even though I wasn't about to show it, that meant a lot to me.

Even so, when Mr. Lee came up to me after class one day and asked if I was interested in taking DS my jaw nearly hit the floor. Me! In Directed Studies! With all the chess club people! Surely he meant Detention, Special. No, he assured me, he actually meant Directed Studies.

My first instinct was to say no. After all, particle physics was not my bag. My math studies had stalled somewhere around grade eight or nine. (To this day I require one of those tip calculators when I go to a restaurant: let this be a warning to all those young people who don't feel math is important.)

"What would I do?" I asked him.

"Well, what are you interested in?" I'm sure part of him must have been worried I was going to propose a course in dating minor drug dealers. But I didn't. I was too astonished by his question.

What was I interested in? The truth is that the worse I'd done in school and in life, the less I was interested in. I'd given up riding and writing, my two main passions. The chess people, the ones who discussed the latest articles from *Harper's* and *The Economist* in hushed tones in the hallways at lunchtime, now *they* had interests. Even I knew that "partying" and drinking were more like avocations than hobbies.

Mr. Lee told me to go away to think about it and that afternoon, I did.

I *was* interested in clothes. A passion for fashion didn't have the same "getting above myself" quality that an interest in, say, micro-economics or golf course design would have. I could bring up the topic of fashion out in the smoking area without hitting a wall of blank, fish-eyed stares that told me I'd crossed yet another line. In fact we often had lively discussions out there about topics such as how acid wash denim was really made and shared the latest news about innovations in curling irons.

So the next time I saw Mr. Lee I announced I wanted to study fashion.

He nodded gravely.

Then I surprised both of us. "Historical fashion. Nineteenth-century costume design," I blurted, thinking of a book I saw once in the library and had glanced at for a minute or two.

His eyebrows rose a bit and he nodded.

"Okay. Write it up."

I spent the evening writing up a proposed course of study. It was the first night I'd spent doing homework in my entire high school career. It was as though merely being asked what I was interested in made me want to come up with something good. It was even sort of fun. Not as fun as getting wasted on wine coolers, obviously, but not bad, either. I proposed spending one term researching nineteenth-century fashions and one term actually making a reproduction of a ball gown from the era. The fact that I (a) had no research skills whatsoever and (b) couldn't sew didn't stop me. I was going to be in DS! We DS types were not afraid to take on a challenge!

Our first DS meeting consisted of me on one side of the room, reeking of cigarette smoke, low self-esteem, and perm solution, and all the smartest kids in grade eleven on the other. I was sure my presence rattled them. What kind of meritocracy allowed a smoking area C student into the ranks? The DS kids weren't mean to my face. By that time, I'd moved fairly solidly into the ranks of the "fairly popular." I went to all the parties and had pretty friends and dated older guys. Instead, they adopted a cautious, slightly soothing manner with me, as though I was an unpredictable and none-too-bright animal, like a young badger or a yearling moose that someone had very inappropriately brought to a party.

Among themselves they had considerable camaraderie. Mark, a tall, dark-haired, round-shouldered boy, teased Samantha, the serious, white-haired editor of the student paper, about her plan to study bias in the media coverage of the federal election. He teased her about her fondness for "soft science." I was appalled. These people made jokes about soft science? What in the fuck was soft science? And what were they going to think when I announced I wanted to study fashion design for a year?

Mark, emboldened by his flirtation, actually spoke to me. "I hope you're pursuing something a bit more quantifiable," he joshed. The people around him shrank visibly, probably concerned that I didn't know what quantifiable meant and, maddened by frustration, would physically attack him. They weren't far off.

But before I could say anything, Mr. Lee took control. He introduced each of us and described our projects. Art would be studying neuroscience; Tina: Japanese calligraphy; Samantha: media studies; Matt: astrophysics. Christopher was going to put Wordsworth in perspective. Bing: economic recovery in postwar Germany. And Susan: nineteenth-century costume design and its social relevance.

As he mentioned my topic, I looked from face to face. No

one appeared all that impressed by my intellectual ambition, but no one laughed out loud either. It was as though my self-esteem, thirsting through a desert of alcohol-related escapades, had been administered a life-saving sip of water.

Over the course of that year I read about the insane yet telling history of fashion and what it reveals about women's roles in society. I struggled to learn basic sewing skills and spent every extra penny (other than those needed to keep my hair in a state of advanced permed-ness and to buy enough booze to get started on the weekends—boyfriends always provided the booze to finish us off) to buy the equipment and materials to make my enormous reproduction ball gown. I enlisted the help of a whole host of women, from the local seamstress to the public librarian, all of whom became quite fascinated by the subject.

I also got to know my fellow DS students and soon began to appreciate the fact that I didn't have to dumb down my vocabulary around them or pretend to be stupid to amuse them. That was something I'd learned to do in my early years at middle school to avoid the dreaded accusation: "Why do you always got to use such big words?"

The Directed Studies kids were so far outside my social circle they might have been my parents' friends. But I grew to like several of them and they seemed to like me.

During the presentation at the end of the year, Christopher put Wordsworth into perspective (turns out he was pretty important). Tina gave a demonstration of Japanese brushwork. Matt talked about what he'd learned about astrophysics. And I came out on stage in a reproduction of a nineteenth-century ball gown complete with velvet bodice fastened by dozens of tiny buttons. The skirt was held out by a crinoline the size of a two-man dome tent and had a hidden pulley system to raise and lower different layers of jewel-toned satin. I talked about how upper-class women were put on pedestals as untouchable symbols of femininity and how their fashions made them literally remote. (I thought, but chose not to mention, that my tendency to projectile-vomit during benders had the same basic effect.) I discussed how during the Extravagant Period, fashion influenced architecture. Doors were made wider to accommodate the giant skirts. Women at the time wore dead birds and insects in their hair as decorations. I talked about how women drank vinegar to increase their pallor and did all kinds of other unhealthy things that made them fit a senseless standard of beauty. It was all very understandable in the eighties milieu. When the talk was over, I had an A in Directed Studies (the only one in my high school career) and had decided to go to fashion design school after I graduated.

The dream of going to college and the entire experience probably kept me in school. It made me realize that even though my lifestyle was fairly out of control, I could still relate to people who didn't party like their lives depended on it. And the fashion school goal was actually achievable, unlike a goal of going to university. I learned this from Mr. Lee's wife, who was the guidance and career counsellor. She helped me find an institution with achievably low standards. The best thing of all was that the school was in Toronto, which, I was fairly sure, was big enough to cure me.

11

The College Months

WHEN MY FLIGHT landed in Toronto, I was greeted by a slender, soft-focus blond woman. She worked for the fashion design college I'd enrolled in, and simply being in her company while I waited for my inexpensive but brand new suitcases made me feel good. This, I thought, was the new me. The *urban* me. The me who was greeted at the airport by nicely appointed blond ladies.

As she drove us along Highway 401 to the student cooperative where I'd be living, I could practically feel myself changing, growing, and getting better and better. I knew no one in this city of two and a half million people, and I'd never felt more alive to the possibilities of life. I stared, exhilarated, at the high-rises that crowded the freeway and at the endless lanes of traffic streaming around us. I was going to start fresh. This wasn't going to be like the time I moved to Salmon Arm.

There are probably people in the witness protection program who feel less relieved to get out of town than I did when I moved from Smithers to Toronto. I knew I wouldn't make the same mistakes again. I was going to be a better person. Maybe even all I could be. I was going to fulfill my inner destiny, which was to be a cutting-edge fashionable person who lived in a major city. No longer would I be the girl who drank too much at parties. The girl who'd been flailing from one crisis to another since she was thirteen. The problem had been my environment. It hadn't allowed me to flourish. But in Toronto all things were possible. Heck, after I got my fashion design career underway, I might even start writing again. Probably get another horse and start to compete and probably go to the Olympics. I would start drinking like a lady or at least not like a guttersnipe. Surely, being in a world-class city like Toronto would do the trick. During a stopover in Calgary, I'd bought myself some wide-legged plaid pants and had my hair spiral-permed. I was already different!

I experienced a moment of fear when we pulled up to the house and knocked on the door. No one else was home. I took the keys that had been mailed to me and opened the door. The lady helped me carry my luggage into the Victorian brownstone. The grand old house had been carved up into sixteen separate bedrooms. There was a kitchen (dirty) on the main floor and bathrooms (also dirty) on the second and third floors. It was, I thought, the nicest house I'd ever seen. There were very few brick buildings in the northern interior of British Columbia. I'd never seen a house so solid. And so old! The floors were hardwood rather than linoleum or carpet. There were mouldings! Never mind that the hardwood floors were scratched and little nails popped out here and there and the mouldings were covered in flaking paint. I took a few steps and knew instantly I was meant to walk on hardwood floors, even if there were quite a few silverfish underfoot.

"Are you going to be okay here by yourself?" asked the nice lady as I stood in the middle of the foyer staring around me with wonder-filled eyes.

I nearly laughed out loud. If I hadn't been so overwhelmed by the classiness of my new situation I might have. I wanted to tell her that I was going to be fine for the first time in my life. Instead

I simply thanked her. When she left, I went upstairs to my new room, on the third floor. It had a sloping ceiling and two beds. I would have a roommate, which was going to be a great novelty and adventure like in those books about boarding schools that I loved to read. My roommate wouldn't know any more about me than anyone else in Toronto. She wasn't going to know about my tarnished reputation. She was going to see a girl from B.C. with an undeniable vivaciousness that matched her wicked new spiral-permed curls. We were probably going to become best and lifelong friends!

Once I'd decided which bed to take, leaving my new roommate the good one because I was now a thoughtful person who did that sort of thing, I decided to explore the neighbourhood. A small-town resident from birth, I was not a natural urban navigator, so I proceeded cautiously. I left the house, making sure the door was locked behind me, and walked around one block. I was relieved to find myself back in front of the right house after four left turns. Next, I ventured two blocks, then three. Each time I found myself back in front of the house, my confidence grew. I was walking around a major city!

On one of my circuits, I noticed that I'd been passing a liquor store. I'd been so focused on not getting irretrievably lost that I hadn't paid attention, but on that trip the store seemed to leap out at me.

What if guests stopped by my new room? I should have something to offer them. What if I got invited to a party? I couldn't show up empty-handed. For all I knew, there might be an official cocktail hour before dining hall.

I ducked into the liquor store and looked at the shelves. I could get a six-pack of beer. But a full case was really a better deal. I picked up a box of Labatt Blue, showed my ID, which the clerk examined very carefully because I looked approximately twelve, especially with my enormous head of fake curls and new clown pants. Then I struggled to carry the beer out of the store and the rest of the way home. The case was heavy and didn't match my outfit, but I persevered.

When I opened the front door, fighting to maintain my grip on my beer, I noticed someone behind me. Another student. Finally.

I held open the door for him while I stared at the floor. (My new confidence didn't extend to meeting a stranger's eyes.) Then I climbed the stairs to my third-floor bedroom. About halfway up the first landing, I realized the man I'd let in was right behind me. Nearly touching me. A glance back told me a few things at once. The man was probably not a student. If he was, he was an extremely mature older student, aged fifty-eight or so, and it looked as though he'd spent his summer vacation sleeping under a park bench. By averting my eyes when I let him in, I'd missed the long, tangled beard, the unkempt and filthy hair under the toque, and the layer upon layer of reeking clothing, complete with bits of newspapers sticking out here and there. The man was a homeless person! I'd heard about those!

I gave a little scream and accelerated up the stairs, the case of beer banging against my legs. I made it up two flights of stairs in about four steps, as though I had a jet pack on my back. Another few leaps and I was at the door of my new room and working the locks. With superhuman dexterity, I let myself and my beer inside, slammed the door, and locked it behind me. I stood panting and listened for noises from the homeless invader or very mature student on the other side. When I heard nothing, I put the case of beer down on my desk.

After trying for a few minutes to think what to do, I decided that the best course of action was to have a drink. I opened one of the bottles and drank half of it. Then I went over to the window and leaned out. A couple walked along the sidewalk below.

"Excuse me," I shouted. "There's someone in the house. I mean, I think there's a homeless man in here."

The couple looked up to where I was leaning out of the window.

"Can you see if he's still here?" I asked.

"Well," said the young man, "I guess we could."

"Why don't you call the police?" asked the woman.

The two of them were remarkably unfazed by this third-floor request for assistance.

"I don't have a phone. I'm not from here," I shouted down. My enormous spiral perm was probably evidence of that.

As I watched, the couple walked to the front door and disappeared from view. A few seconds later, their heads reappeared. The man looked up at my window.

"We can't get in," he said. "The door's locked."

"Oh," I replied. "That's right."

"Can you let us in?"

It dawned on me that I didn't know these two any better than I did that homeless guy who was probably hiding outside my room right now, thinking of all the things he'd like to do to an out-of-towner in plaid pants. I'd read literally dozens of books about serial killers. I knew the score.

Who to trust?

I ducked back into the room and quickly finished off the beer. Then I returned to the window.

"Never mind," I said. "I'm fine." Then I belched, loud and wet.

"You sure?" asked the girl.

I nodded down at them. Finally, they walked off down the street and I sat on my bed to wait. I reflected that it had been a stressful day so far. A person, even an urban one, might need a second drink to take the edge off. So I had one. Then, because I was trapped in my room by a possible serial killer, I had a third.

Half an hour later, or maybe longer, I heard voices and footsteps outside in the hall.

"Hello?" I said, from behind my locked door.

"Hello?" It was a young man's voice. Either the homeless guy sounded much younger than he was or some other students had arrived.

"Hi?" I said.

"Hi?"

I didn't know whether to keep shouting hello through the door. The sounds of laughter increased. Music began to play. Guns N' Roses. I decided to risk it. I opened the door and peeked out. In the room next door, I could see a few guys about my age milling around. They did not appear to be street people.

One poked his head out of the room and saw me staring. "Hey," he said. He had a nice smile, short black hair, and freckled dark skin. "Are you the girl from B.C.?"

"Susan," I said.

"Cool," he said. "I'm John. The house manager."

I felt like throwing myself into his arms with relief.

A red-haired boy poked his head out from John's room.

"I'm Bart. You want a beer?" he asked.

Did I? After what I'd been through! I decided not to mention that I'd had a few drinks in my own room already and that I had hidden the rest of the beer under my bed.

Fifteen minutes later, after I'd shared a couple of drinks with them, I finally remembered to call my mother to let her know I'd arrived.

John lent me his phone.

"Hi, Mom. Yeah, I'm fine. No, it's great here. I love it. I'm totally at home already."

And I was.

AT FIRST COLLEGE LIFE seemed like it was designed with me in mind. Or at least with heavy drinking in mind. I had the great good fortune to end up living in a house with a group of committed drinkers. John and Craig (business at U of T) and Bart (forestry at U of T) spent a lot of time devising elaborate drinking rituals. These included Gin and Tonic Tuesdays and Sticky Wicket Wednesdays (ten-cent wings and cheap draft at a local pub). My housemates were very welcoming and seemed to find my northern drinking habits refreshingly unfeminine and easy to relate to.

"Wow," they said after our first night out when I matched them two for one. "You drink like a guy!"

The admiration in their voices was unmistakable. Some of the other girls who went out with us drank, but none with the avidity I did. John was from a small suburb on the outskirts of Toronto. He was into heavy metal. I knew plenty of metal guys back home, but they hadn't been university-bound. I had no idea the two things were compatible. In Toronto I discovered the suburban, brainiac metalhead. Nice boys who loved loud music and certain aspects of the metal lifestyle. They were into the music, but they maintained some perspective on the whole scene. When we saw metal groupies at clubs, squeezed into Day-Glo tube tops, huge hair teased to impossible heights, hoping to get close to the musicians, these boys knew enough to find it funny. John, especially, was always getting embarrassed on other people's behalf. But drinking was part of the metal scene that they embraced wholeheartedly.

In addition to my excellent drinking skills, my new friends appreciated my taste in music. I made John a mix tape and he couldn't contain himself. He said it was the kind of mix he might have made himself.

I basked in his praise. Later, after I'd given him a few more tapes, his enthusiasm was tempered by the realization that I basically made the same tape over and over in different combinations, a practice I continue to this day.

Fashion school became something I did when I wasn't drinking with my new friends.

The first indication that I was an outlier came from Ed, a self-possessed Italian-Canadian from Montreal and the most mature member of our campus co-op crew. He watched me eat takeout instead of what was on offer at the dining hall, shop for clothes, and switch halfway through the night from cheap draft beer to pricey hard liquor. One day he said, "You're going to run out of money if you keep spending like that."

I looked at him like he was crazy. A few rye and Cokes weren't about to exhaust my enormous student loan. So what if I was attending a college notable for its low barrier to entry and high tuition fees, which were over twice as much as my housemates attending university paid? In addition to the loan, my mother was sending me a small allowance each month. I was rich! I had never been allowed to handle any significant amount of money before and it went directly to my head. I found the prime shopping districts in Toronto and showed no restraint. One memorable afternoon, I bought an all-green outfit of paisley rayon blouse, matching short skirt, thigh-high socks, green velvet slippers with a fake family crest on the toe, and green cardigan. The outfit cost more than my monthly expenses and made me look like a giant zucchini, but I convinced myself that as an aspiring fashion designer, it was important that I develop a signature or brand, if you will. Mine was going to be all-one-colour outfits.

And as the weeks wore on and I made the switch from draft to hard liquor earlier each evening, my money seemed to evaporate. So did the illusion that I fit in with my new friends and that I was just another high-spirited social drinker.

After a pleasant interlude in which I acted like a cheery drunk, I started undergoing the personality changes that had always marked my drinking. After a few drinks I'd get nasty and aggressive.

I was strongly attached to the idea that I was just a wild and crazy college student like everybody else, but that image became harder to maintain when I started doing things like falling down, dead drunk, on a busy sidewalk on Bloor Street in the middle of the afternoon, while wearing my all-green outfit. I'll never forget the sensation of people walking by me and, in some cases, over me. The few that looked at me wore expressions of pity tinged with revulsion. Not the sort of looks a vivacious (if slightly wild) college coed hoped to produce.

One night we were running down Bloor Street on a pub crawl, and Ed made some teasing comment about my not-exactly-Ivy-League educational institution. I was seized with a rare school spirit. I couldn't let him get away with the slur! The stores and bars had just put out their garbage for the collectors to pick up the next morning. Possessed by alcohol-induced strength, I hoisted up a black garbage bag and pitched it at Ed. My aim was not true. The bag went sailing out into the street and exploded like a bomb onto a passing car. It turned out that the bag had been full of bottles. Worse news was that the vehicle I'd hit was black and white and had a rack of lights on top. Stunned (and drunk), I froze.

In an instant, my companions scattered and took off running. Everyone else on the street, students and bar crawlers mostly, cried out as one.

"Oooooh shit!"

I waited for a good five minutes while the cops turned the car around in the heavy traffic and came back. I walked unsteadily toward the car. Instantly, we were surrounded by every drunken asshole in a four-mile radius.

"Don't arrest her!"

"Arrest me!"

"Police brutality!"

The cops were so surprised that I'd waited, swaying gently like some upended sea cucumber, that they didn't seem to know what to do with me.

"Sorry," I said. "I didn't mean to, uh, hit your car. The bag slipped."

The officer was steamed, but perhaps because I was young and had hair that looked like a bad wig and wore an outfit that made me look like a garden vegetable, he took pity.

"Nice friends you got. Ran away and left you."

I didn't reply because I was trying not to vomit down the side of the car. I'd never spent a night in the drunk tank, and had no desire to start now.

"Sorry," I said.

The cop leaned further out the passenger-side window. He ignored the crowd and spoke directly to me.

"Maybe you should think about drinking a bit less."

I blinked, startled as though he'd clapped the handcuffs on me.

"Police brutality!" shouted a drunk guy from across the street at no one in particular.

Police brutality indeed.

BY THE TIME Christmas break rolled around, I was almost as uncomfortable in Toronto as I'd been in Smithers. I was doing very badly in school. I didn't have the worst marks, because a few of the people in my program spoke almost no English, but I was near the bottom. I'd made myself unpopular with many of my housemates with my unpredictable behaviour and tendency to come home drunk and make so much noise I woke everyone up.

"Thoughtlessness, thy name is Juby," a student of classics muttered in my direction one morning.

My drinking had completely outstripped that of my heavy metal friends. They cut back in order to focus on classes. Cutting back was an impossible dream for me. Moving to Toronto and going to fashion design school hadn't fixed what ailed me. My drinking was worse than ever. At least at home, I'd been surrounded by other people who drank like it was an Olympic sport. In Toronto, surrounded by productive, functional, clear-minded, and middle-class students, I felt completely alone. Still, I wasn't willing to face the reality that I couldn't pull off normal no matter where I lived or what I did. I clung on to the last scraps of the college dream like Kate Winslet gripping that piece of the *Titanic*. Only less cutely, obviously.

Rather than assess the fact that my drinking had made yet another place hideously uncomfortable, I focused on the idea of going back to Smithers at Christmas and playing the part of the triumphant urbanite. I would show everyone that I was no longer a slightly out-of-control piss tank, but rather a successful fashion design student and big city dweller. I hadn't always been the most popular person in my hometown, but that was because the people there had not understood that I was suffering from fish-out-of-water syndrome. The big city was my water. Smithers just didn't get me. Et cetera.

As soon as I arrived, I started making the rounds of old friends and hitting every Christmas party I could find. I wore my new Toronto clothes, including my clown pants and zucchini outfit, and tried to show by word and deed that I was a more sophisticated woman. I was no longer the train wreck I'd been when I left.

By New Year's Eve I'd been drunk almost every night for almost two weeks. I found that my friends who'd stayed behind had committed themselves wholeheartedly to the party life and were embroiled in the kinds of incredibly messy relationships nineteen- and twenty-year-olds excel at. Everybody was cheating on everybody and I felt kind of sorry for myself that I'd missed it all. The only time I felt slightly vindicated in my life choices was when people told me they admired my bravery in wearing such strange clothes.

Looking at pictures taken that Christmas, I can see that I didn't look quite so much the stylish college girl as I'd hoped. There's a shot of my mother and me standing outside her new apartment. She'd moved into it after divorcing my stepfather the year before. The two of us had gone out to get a "Christmas branch" to make things look more festive. I'm standing against a snowy backdrop, which serves to make my face look even more sallow and bloated. My spiral perm is half grown out. I look ten years older than I was and more haggard than collegiate.

I was due to return to Toronto on New Year's Day, so I felt it was important that I go out with a bang. Leave them with their mouths hanging open. Show how it's done when you live in Toronto. Et cetera.

I hit the bottle of Crown Royal early and hard. When the coke came out, I was first in line. Coke had a tendency to make me violent, but it also allowed me to drink more and for longer, so I snarfled up as much as I could.

By the time we hit the bar, a decrepit old cabaret populated mostly by the local rubbies and young drinkers "slumming it," I was flying. We were confronted by the girlfriend of one of the boys one of my friends was sleeping with. Names were called. Threats were uttered. As a fashion design student I felt it was my duty to intervene.

I inserted myself between the combatants and when the cheated-upon girlfriend complained, I lobbed a few wobbly, coke-fuelled punches at her. Next thing I knew I was being carried, none too gently, off the sticky dance floor by a bouncer. He was not swayed by my beauty or the urbanity of my clothing.

As I was being dragged past the stage, I saw the musicians glance at each other as they kept playing. Something told me they weren't thinking, "Wow. She must be from Toronto!"

A moment later I was on my hands and knees on the frozen sidewalk.

After that, I remember nothing. The blackout lasted until my mother woke me up the next day to inform me that I had a phone call. It was early afternoon and I tried not to notice when my mother wrinkled her nose at how I smelled. In our family, we don't go stating the obvious about people's problems, so she said nothing about the alcoholic off-gassing.

"Phone," she said.

I took the receiver from her with a trembling hand.

"Is this Susan Juby?" asked a girl's voice.

"Yes," I croaked.

"You're fucking dead, you bitch."

My heart began to race like I'd never stopped doing coke.

"I am going to kick your ass. Meet us behind the Civic Centre at six tonight or you'll be sorry."

I hung up the phone. My mother stared at me with a quizzical expression.

"Who was that?"

"Just a friend," I said.

Four hours later, I was huddled in my seat on a tiny plane that was battling its way through a terrible snowstorm on its way from Smithers to the Vancouver Airport, where I was supposed to catch my connecting flight to Toronto. I imagined the caller waiting to beat me up behind the Civic Centre. She'd be surrounded by shivering spectators. Nineteen years old, a fashion design student living in Toronto, and entire crowds of people still wanted to beat me up. I was going to be forty-four and still getting into fights every weekend. Why did these things keep happening to me?

As the plane bucked its way through the storm, the flimsy curtain that separated the eight or so passengers from the cockpit rose and fell. Sometimes the curtain flapped high enough that I could see dark sweat circles through the young pilot's white dress shirt.

If we survive this flight, I promised myself, *I'm going to do better this term. I'm going to stop spending money and I'm going to cut back on my drinking. This time, I'm going to pull it together. I will*

never do cocaine again, and I will focus on my school work. I will
be good.

Of course, as soon as I got back to Toronto, I picked up where I left off, drinking myself into a blackout a couple of nights a week and racing through the scant remains of my student loan. Later, I heard that not long after my escape from Smithers, the same little plane I'd taken crashed flying the same route and killed everyone on board.

12

When the End Is Nigh

HERE'S WHAT HAPPENED when I returned to Toronto. I failed to pay my tuition on time and was asked to leave my fashion design college. They said I should think about exploring "other avenues for my talents." To celebrate the end of my college career, I got very drunk with some unsuspecting classmates and dragged them to a male strip club. After I finished impressing everyone with my ability to guzzle multiple nine-dollar Long Island iced teas in just over an hour, I tripped and fell down two flights of stairs and rolled out onto Yonge Street. I think I may have attacked one of my companions when she came back to my house, where she was supposed to be staying. This is only the dimmest of memories. She was gone when I got up, and I never heard from her again.

When I awoke I found three small plastic flasks of vodka, one hidden in my purse, one in my coat pocket, and another tucked into my winter hat. I had no recollection of buying them. This was happening more and more. When I came to after one of my binges, I would find alcohol stashed everywhere. There would be stray cans of beer in my dresser drawers, airplane bottles in my shoes, and mickeys in random pockets of my knapsack. I was terrified that I'd have to stop drinking once I'd started. For some reason, this booze hoarding didn't strike me as unhappy housewife/

bad dad alcoholic behaviour, because I was drunk when I bought the backup bottles and so it didn't count. Also, judging from the untouched evidence, I never seemed to remember them after I tucked them away. I was like a smelling-impaired dog burying a bone, not like a true alkie.

Having washed out of a not terribly demanding college, an amazing feat on its own, I began drinking alone and going out by myself with no money in my pocket. The alternative was to stay home, alone and sober, and that would have forced me to acknowledge that I was an unemployed fashion school dropout, basically hiding out in my student co-op, waiting for someone to realize that I was no longer a student. There had always been at least one part of my life I could control. I might be a mess on weekends, but during the week I was as tightly wound as a new Slinky. I made sure my shoes matched my shirt and my purse. But even that control was slipping. There were fewer and fewer functional moments.

I started coming out of blackouts (it felt like suddenly sobering up) in strange, dingy bars in unfamiliar parts of the city surrounded by people I didn't know. Usually sketchy-looking men. I'd seen *The Accused*. I knew this was a pretty terrible idea.

Another unwelcome development was that I'd started trying to off myself almost every time I got drunk. My attempts usually involved giving my wrists a close shave with a plastic razor while sitting slumped on the bathroom floor, tears running down my face as I cried silently. I also took to wandering into the little park across from my house and waiting for the Scarborough rapist (later revealed to be the horror show called Paul Bernardo) to come and get me. The park was about the size of a large area rug, and I would stagger outside and lie on the single bench plunked down in the middle. When sober, I, like many women in the Toronto area, was afraid to go out after dark. But drunk, I was capable of anything.

I proved totally incompetent at suiciding myself, but when I sobered up I started to worry that by some unlucky fluke I might actually succeed.

This drastic escalation in my drinking took its toll. When my housemates would go out for breakfast the morning after a party, they usually asked if I'd like to go along. I never did because I couldn't. While they were eating cheap eggs benedict and talking about their escapades from the night before, I would be huddled out on the third-floor fire escape, smoking, every muscle shaking independently and uncontrollably, and doing my best to ignore the mild DTs that I'd started experiencing every time I sobered up from a binge. I ignored the flashes of movement that darted in and out of my peripheral vision; the dark figures descending the walls and swooping flashes of birds in the hallways. None of it was real.

It was very hard to pretend that I was still having fun.

Even more devastating than the physical trauma my drinking was causing was the collapse of the barriers that I'd erected to keep my drinking life separate from the rest of my life. Probably no one, even back in high school, had any idea how much I drank or how it affected me. Part of that was because I kept such a tight lid on myself when sober. I was shy, as noted, and profoundly uptight. When I got drunk I came across as more hyper or crazy than drunk. I spent all my sober time trying to make up for my drinking time.

Even during my worst days in Toronto, I'm sure no one I lived with had any idea how sick I was. This is one of the odd things about a certain kind of binge drinker. I didn't drink during the day, generally, and I usually did it with others, so it wasn't as obvious as it might have been. But when my drinking began to infect my sober life in a way that even I, with my bionic powers of denial, couldn't ignore, the end was nigh. The weight of my drinking life was like a house I'd been holding up. It had finally gotten too heavy and was slowly crushing me.

For a few months, my main employment between binges had been holding down a couch in the living room with one or two of the engineering students who never seemed to attend classes. When I was not too hung over, I ate pillow-sized bags of salt and vinegar potato chips. When I was sick, I huddled in my room under many blankets and tried to control the tremors in my hands. When the shaking subsided, I came out and slouched, lumpen, on the sagging sofa in the dark and watched hour after hour of *Star Trek*, wishing fervently that I was aboard the *Enterprise*.

After I'd been out of school for a few months, I somehow got a job at a yarn store. When people asked how I landed it, I told them it was because of my "fashion background." That was a lie. A friend of the family had told the owner that I desperately needed employment. The owner, a somewhat scattered, eccentric woman who wore floor-length sweaters with metallic bits sticking out all over the place, very kindly hired me, in spite of the fact that I couldn't knit. Not one stitch. Knitting was one of the courses at my fashion college, but I'd dropped out before we got to it.

When I got back to being gainfully employed, it was a huge relief. I'd had a job since I was fifteen, and while I was no one's idea of a prize employee, my jobs had allowed me to delude myself that I still had some control over my life.

Working in the tiny storefront, the walls lined with wooden cubbyhole shelving, was like slowly suffocating for eight dollars an hour, eight hours a day. The shelves bulged with yarn. The store was probably cozy during the winter, but in the summer when the temperature regularly soared past thirty degrees and the relentless humidity made it feel at least ten degrees warmer, the air-conditionless store was a lanolin-smelling inferno.

The only thing that made it bearable was my co-worker, Calvin. He was a small, delicately built man, a gifted knitter, weaver, and spinner, although I knew this only from what people said about his work. He was also refreshingly embittered. He was scathing about most of our customers and about the world at large. But he was never anything but kind to me.

Calvin was the first out gay man I'd ever met. He'd been a dancer in the National Ballet as a young man when he was young and had starved himself to make the cut. In the process, he'd developed a severe case of diabetes. Every so often he would lapse into a coma and have to be rushed to the hospital. He was my favourite person, partly because my personality was almost sunny compared to his.

We'd sit sweating at the front counter. Calvin would irritably twitch a Chinese fan in front of his face as though swatting away wasps. When asked, he'd show me the difference between knitting and purling, although he clearly didn't care whether I could do either. When a customer entered the store, his eyes glittered malevolently behind his round glasses. If it was one of the deal-seeking older Italian or Polish ladies from the neighbourhood, he'd be furious in his contempt.

"There are no bargains here," he'd say, shaking in their faces the ball of twenty-dollar silk that they wanted marked down to three dollars. "NO BARGAINS!"

If the customer was one of the cool young women wearing belly-baring outfits of black leggings, cut-off jean shorts, cowboy boots, and tank tops, he'd sit and silently judge them as they moved through the store. When they were gone, he'd mutter things like "Some people really shouldn't wear tights."

If he really had it in for someone, he'd ask me to serve them.

When I wasn't stocking shelves, I spent my time knitting back and forth on pieces of remnant yarn. This, combined with the fact that I worked in a yarn store, led customers to believe I knew something about knitting.

"I'm curious about this pattern. Can you show me where the cable stitching moves back into stocking stitch?" they'd ask.

I didn't want to admit that I was more likely to start spontaneously speaking Farsi than I was to be able to interpret a knitting pattern, so I would carefully study the sheet of paper or book and make a lot of faces meant to indicate fierce concentration. After the two of us had been standing around long enough for it to get embarrassing, I'd say something like "This is kind of a weird pattern." Or "Jeez, I've never seen one like this before."

The customers, to their credit, never pressed. They never demanded to know why such an incompetent was working in a knitting store. One look at Calvin, his lips pursed with hostility, and they simply left.

I really, really loved Calvin.

He never said anything when I had the shakes. He never commented when I came in reeking of beer and vomit, which I did at least twice a week. He made no disparaging remarks about my dead-broke fashions or untended hair. Even the day I got the unexpected visitor, he never said a word.

It happened one sweltering afternoon a month or so after I'd started at Yarn Inc. I sat at the counter, knitting back and forth on the same pieces of yarn I'd been torturing for the past several days.

My process was to change colours every inch or so, make several unsightly mistakes along the way, then unravel the whole thing, encouraged only by Calvin's comment about my "adventurous colour sense." I knit like I drank, with a relentless monotony and uniformly poor results.

When asked, I told people my "thing" was going to be a pillowcase, because my "thing" was roughly rectangular. At least most of it was. Sometimes, when I got distracted or was extremely worse for wear, the "thing" came out octagonal or even oval.

On the day in question, Calvin sat behind me eating Chinese takeout from the place down the block. I was in charge of customer service, which wasn't hard because it was nearly thirty-five degrees outside and forty inside the store and no one was thinking about knitwear.

I was therefore surprised when a slightly underfed-looking young man entered the store. The fact that he was male made him noteworthy. The fact that he was young and a trifle weaselly made him more so.

He walked right up to the counter. He had a question. Great. Just my luck.

"Hey," he said.

"Uh, can I help you?"

"I know you," he said. There was an accusing tone in his voice and alarm bells began to go off in every part of my body. As a committed blackout drinker, I worried constantly about running into the people I met on benders, people I had no hope of remembering when I sobered up.

I forced myself not to look back at Calvin, who I knew couldn't help but overhear.

"Really," I said, keeping it noncommittal.

"I met you last weekend."

"Yeah?" I said. My heart thudded in an ominous way. A heart-attack-inducing way.

"Do you remember me?"

Oh Christ. Not this. Chances were that we'd been introduced by a mutual friend and exchanged two sentences. But we might also have talked the night away. We might have made out. We might have, god help me, had sex. We could have gotten married and adopted an orphan from Romania for all I knew. I was that kind of blackout drinker.

"Hmmmm," I said. The layer of sweat that had lain on my skin all day turned cold and clammy.

"You don't remember at all, do you?" he said.

As when pretending to understand knitting patterns, I attempted to look thoughtful. Like there was a chance I'd get the memory back. Or grow a new one.

"You told me you were a veterinary student," said the boy, who had an insistent Adam's apple that bobbed distractingly all over the front of his throat when he spoke.

I froze.

This was an unwelcome reminder that lately, when drinking, I'd taken to making up far-fetched achievements for myself, probably to compensate for the fact that my twenty-year-old life was beginning to feel like a bit of a washout.

Several times I'd employed the "This is the first time I've ever gotten drunk" lie, which served to make me feel like less of an alcoholic and more of a naïf. Then there were the career lies, which had begun shortly after I'd been asked to leave my fashion design college. I didn't tell these lies in a fun, ironic way either. I told them when I was drunk with a dead seriousness that made them seem even more pathetic when I had the misfortune to be reminded of them later. I'd recently told a group of frat boys at a bar that I was an heir to a "small appliances fortune." When asked which appliances, I suggested I was one of the General Electric family.

And now here I was confronted with the spectre of imaginary veterinary medical studies. The walls of my carefully compartmentalized life were coming down.

"Oh really?" I said, giving a sickly little laugh and trying to decide whether I should deny everything. Laugh it off? Brazen it out? Say the yarn store gig was just something I did when I wasn't at the zoo working with the rhinos or doing pro-bono autopsies on road kill?

"Why would you tell me something like that?" he asked.

This guy was a nightmare. No one should ever confront an alcoholic about the idiotic shit she says while drunk. It's like an unwritten law. Gossip about what a drunken whore she is. Dismiss her as a crazy. But don't go confronting her directly. That is just not cool. In my circle, it was completely unheard of.

What was his problem? It didn't sound like I'd punched him or anything, which was another thing I'd started doing to strangers with increasing frequency.

"Ha, ha," I said. My face was on fire.

"That's a really weird thing to do," said the guy.

He should talk, I thought. No normal person would come in here, hounding me about things I'd said while drunk at a party. I was trapped, humiliated. On the verge of bursting into tears or falling off my stool and impaling myself on a knitting needle.

Suddenly, Calvin was standing beside me. He wasn't very tall, so at first I hadn't noticed.

"You want to buy something?" he asked my inquisitor.

"No," said the boy.

"Goodbye then," said Calvin.

The boy gave me another sullen look and then turned and walked back out into the bright, dirty afternoon. Calvin rested a hand lightly on my shoulder before going back and finishing his lunch. He never said another word about my visitor.

That afternoon, when Calvin went to run an errand, I called a number in the phone book and asked where the nearest meeting was.

OH HELL, I guess there's something else I should mention here. The visit from my unremembered acquaintance wasn't the only thing that precipitated my call for help. Of course it wasn't. There'd been seven years of traumas and humiliations connected with my drinking. But there was another final straw that I hesitate to mention because it sounds cliché or at least terrifically suspect, like the kind of shoddy psychologizing practised by some disreputable therapist on *Law & Order*. Many months after I made that phone call, I found myself attending a workshop about sexual harassment. I'd volunteered to write and implement a harassment policy for my housing co-op. This in itself was strong evidence of the personal changes I'd undergone. Previously, I'd have more likely been the target of such a policy.

At the time, awareness about sexual harassment was sweeping the campuses of North America. As minor-key social progressives, we at the co-op weren't about to be left out. The course was conducted by a pair of Birkenstocked women's rights activists from the University of Toronto. They told us about the circumstances under which most women on campuses are assaulted.

The rosy-faced woman with white-blond hair said, "It almost always involves alcohol."

Her fellow workshop leader, nodded. "When women are drunk, they feel responsible."

As I sat in the middle of the room, I felt a dreadful awareness settle over me. It was accompanied by an image of myself, wasted, as usual. I was sitting in someone's bedroom in the house next door to mine. There were maybe seven or eight other people in there, some of whom were playing guitar and singing. I was legless, which was unusual. I'd always been quite ambulatory, even when I was very drunk. I was having trouble seeing and even more trouble moving. Somehow, I made my way into the bathroom, which was located up a flight of stairs. I managed to get inside, but before I could close the door, someone came in behind me and locked the door. It was the tall, argumentative guy who lived in another division of the co-op. I'd always made a point of avoiding him before. Something about him made me uncomfortable. His looming face was the end of the memory, which trailed off into a terrible, terrible feeling.

In the past, I'd had barely consensual intimate encounters, to put it euphemistically. It often seemed like less work to go along than to get up and leave. But this memory was of something very different. A few months after that workshop, I was at a Halloween party for the whole co-op. I happened to glance out the window and I saw the same guy carrying a limp girl into a taxi. She was dressed in a cat suit, and if she wasn't passed out, she was certainly close. I pushed through the crowd and ran outside, but by that time they were gone. Was that girl his date? Had he picked her up at the party? What was in store for her? I had no way to know and no way to prove what I suspected.

Had I been assaulted or was my memory some terrible manifestation of all my ambivalence about the things I did and that happened to me when I drank? I don't know. I will never know. All I can say is that after that night I could no longer pretend that anything about my life was manageable or controllable or safe.

part II

A QUITTER'S STORY

13

The Kindness of Oldheads

WELL, THEY WERE CERTAINLY OLD. A little rough around the edges, raspy voiced. Reeking of kindness and a certain, rough-hewn tolerance, just like I remembered. But they were also quite ancient in a way that was impossible to ignore.

When I was a kid I'd been to dozens of meetings with my adoptive father. What I remember about those meetings was the chain-smoking, raspy-voiced ladies who stood at the podiums at the front of the linoleum-floored rooms. The no-frills decor and the permanent cloud cover of smoke hanging over everything made those rooms feel like home.

Now I was at a meeting for myself and by myself. I was at least twenty years younger than anyone else in the room.

I'd taken some care getting ready and had dressed in clothes that didn't draw too much attention. My spiral perm had nearly grown out, but the ends were violently corkscrewed and split. My hair was two-toned, dark brown at the roots and orangey-blond at the tips. It had been months since I'd had the money to get it done. My face had been swollen since my last bender, the one I'd thought was finally going to kill me. I'd read somewhere that models who partied too hard sometimes put slices of cucumber on their eyes to take away swelling. The communal fridge at my student co-op didn't have any cucumbers, so before the meeting I put two pieces of old green pepper over my eyes for half an hour. That had accomplished nothing but making me smell like a stir-fry.

I'd recently chipped one of my front teeth, either in a fight or while opening a beer bottle. So I wore darker lipstick to compensate.

When I called the number in the phone book, the person I spoke to said there was a meeting near where I lived. She said I should go to it. That it would make me feel better. It turned out that the meeting was held in the church just down the street. The proximity of the meeting seemed like a sign of some sort. Still, I didn't want the sixteen other students I lived with to know where I was going. I already felt like a fraud, since I was no longer technically a student. My co-op hadn't figured that out yet, and I wasn't about to inform them and risk getting evicted. Anyway, I hadn't exactly *failed* out of school. The decision had basically been mutual.

I walked all the way around the block and came at the church from the opposite direction so no one from my house would see me going in. The room, which I found by following a series of cryptic, handmade signs, was upstairs in the church and located at the end of a narrow hallway, lined with navy blue carpeting, gritty with accumulated dirt and smoke and guilt.

I walked into the low-ceilinged little room and tried to look confident, as though I were just dropping by, looking for new avenues for my talents. My self-esteem was almost entirely denuded, but I still had a few scrawny branches left.

"Hi," said a few of the six people already seated around the table.

Their greetings seemed excessively warm, and I was instantly suspicious that they'd been hoping an interesting young person like myself would come along. I sat down and spotted—my god!—was that pity in their eyes? Directed at me? Sweet Jesus. I was inspiring pity in people like this! The snap of the remaining twigs of my self-esteem was almost audible.

People recited some things off of cards and then started "sharing around the table." When it was my turn and they looked at me with their sympathy-filled eyes and asked me if I wanted to share, I lost it. I managed to say my name and then broke into wracking sobs. No one said anything to me. They just let me cry. I figured that meant they were unprepared for a disaster on my scale. They'd never seen anything like it!

I felt so bad for them that I even managed to stop crying. And when the meeting was over and a skinny, grey-faced lady of indeterminate age came over to tell me about how she'd spent the last few years living behind a Dumpster, quite of few of my worst suspicions were confirmed. She asked me several times to call her and handed me her phone number, which she'd written on the back of a pamphlet. I flashed on an image of me bringing her, the recently homeless lady, to a party at my student residence. There'd be the Ph.D. candidate from Ghana, the one who spent his weekends slow-cooking goats he'd picked up at Kensington Market; the literature students from Ireland, who partied like it was their life mission but, unlike me, functioned the next day; the girls at teachers' college, who seemed to all have cute bangs and clear moral codes. There'd be my heavy metal friends who studied business management at the University of Toronto, and the lone, frighteningly intense medical student with creepy eyes. And then me, the small-town girl who'd managed to fail out of the fashion college that no one had ever heard of, accompanied by a lady who used to live behind a Dumpster. Much as I yearned to be a fearless provocateur, the thought made me blanch.

"Call me if you feel like drinking," the lady from the Dumpster called after me.

"Sure," I said. "I'll do that."

I trotted down the stairs and out onto the street. Once outside, I headed directly away from where I lived and walked a good mile or so before turning around, circling several times to discourage anyone who might be tailing me. But when I was safely back in my room, I found, to my surprise, that I felt marginally better. I had no idea why.

I sat on my bed and took the sweaty pamphlet out of my pocket and read it. It was a questionnaire. And it took me about three seconds to realize that here, at last, was a quiz I could pass.

14

Leaving la Vida Loca

AFTER I'D BEEN GOING to meetings at the church near my house for about a month, some of my paranoia about being relentlessly pursued by the sad old people who went there abated. First of all, they weren't that sad. Or old. They were actually sort of age-appropriate and seemed to have their own friends and lives, which was more than I could say. Second, I noticed that all the advice they'd given me so far had been good. Don't drink one day at a time. If you don't pick up the first drink, you won't get drunk. First things first. All those mindless slogans were surprisingly helpful and not so mindless as I'd thought. Then there was the fact that even though some of my fellow meeting-goers were sort of depressing to look at, due to their advanced ages, and some were straight up annoying and talked for too long about things that were not interesting to me, I seemed to leave every meeting feeling better. For an hour or so, anyway. And that hour was a much-needed break from how I felt the rest of the time, which was volcanically angry. I wasn't sure how long I'd be able to stay sober. At first, I wasn't sure I wanted to, because as soon as I stopped drinking, I developed a bad case of clenched fists and a hateful heart.

When I stopped drinking, I was prepared for life to become deadly dull. Fun, as I'd known it, was over. Forever. There had been a lot of good times. Some of the adventures I had when drinking were outstanding. Booze enabled me to be and to do a lot of things I couldn't on my own. Drinking cut through the fear and the awkwardness. But then it turned on me. The sweet spot, somewhere between drinks two and four, disappeared, and if I drank or tried to get high I would get unpleasantly, paralytically drunk after the first sip. After years of having nearly superhuman tolerance, I suddenly had none. Even drugs didn't seem to work.

The twin fears of being dead and being bored are, for a lot of people, so closely intertwined they are pretty much the same thing. Almost everyone I've spoken to who sobered up in their teens and twenties (and many who did so after) were convinced that sobriety would be only marginally preferable to being dead. That was certainly how I felt. I wasn't quite ready to die, but I had very low expectations for the rest of my life.

So I was prepared for dullness and stultification. What I wasn't prepared for was the rage that consumed me when I sobered up. Being angrily sober was so exhausting that I even tried some of the other things that were suggested in the meetings.

Ask for help in the morning and give thanks at night, said the people. I tried it and it seemed to work. I wasn't too clear on who or what I was asking, but that didn't seem to matter.

I wasn't religious and never had been, except for that year I had myself transferred into the local Catholic school because I thought converting would make people think I was gifted. The nuns had mostly been cranky old birds who treated the few white students in school completely differently from the native kids, which was good for no one. On frigid winter mornings, when the temperature dipped to twenty-five or thirty below zero, the nuns invited the kids from the reserve into the school for a warm breakfast, assuming that they didn't get fed at home, which in some cases was probably true, but in other cases was straight-up insulting. The white kids, no matter what their home situation, were made to stay outside until the bell rang, huddling behind white humps of buried playground equipment and hatching race-based revenge fantasies. The nuns seemed to have a special gift for stoking resentment among the very young, which, in that town in that time, was not needed.

Partly as a result of my early conversion and subsequent abandonment of Catholicism, I'd always found religious people both weak and intimidating. The certainty of the faithful bugged me. Their sense of belonging made me feel worse about myself.

But for all my prejudices, I wasn't opposed to asking the powers that be in the universe for a little help. What could it hurt? I was a thoroughgoing hypocrite in most matters: why not with God?

By Week Four, which was by three weeks the longest I'd gone without getting drunk since I was thirteen, a terrible reality about sobriety was beginning to sink in. I'd thought that I'd stop drinking and my inner nice girl would finally, at long last, emerge. I was convinced that the only thing standing between me and upstanding citizenship was booze and the occasional bump of cocaine. Once I quit drinking I wouldn't be such a hag any more. I wouldn't blow up at people or hate them quite so much. I also hoped I wouldn't hate myself quite so much. Sadly, when sober, I seemed to be the Bitch of Ages.

It turned out that drinking had been the only thing that stood between me and a stark awareness of how crappy everything was. My roommates were unbearable. As the sole sober person in the house, I became acutely aware of how thoughtless they were. Coming home at all hours! Making noise! Leaving the empty juice jug in the fridge! Fucking animals! Never mind the months I'd spent coming home, late and loud. Maybe I'd been a bit of an asshole when I was drinking, but I had an excuse. I was an *alcoholic*. I bet none of these other inconsiderate bastards could say that!

The people in meetings were always talking about how sober people had to leave behind their "old companions." Fine for them. They didn't live with sixteen of their old companions. Also, they didn't mind hanging out with *each other*, which I did. If I didn't spend time with at least some of my old companions, I'd have *no* companions at all. I might have hated many of my housemates (for no good reason), but I wasn't about to stop hanging out with them. As the loneliest, angriest girl in Toronto, I had zero companions to spare.

So night after night, I went to house parties and bars with other inhabitants of the co-op, which was made up of several divisions of houses grouped by the street they were on. I stayed sober. As was probably inevitable, at one of the parties a guy I didn't recognize handed me a freshly opened beer.

"Peace?" he said, hesitantly.

Apparently I'd taken a little swing at him the last time we'd met.

I was so surprised that I took the can.

As I held the cold beer, a thought slithered into my head. *I'll quit drinking tomorrow. Tonight people are handing me open beer. I've been overreacting. I don't need to quit. All I need to do is cut down. Or get married to someone who will help me cut down.* Of course I was trying to rationalize having a drink. The interesting thing was that this was the first time I'd had the chance to do even that. Before, picking up a drink had been completely automatic.

I spent a good minute letting the thought spin in my head like a rotisserie chicken. Then I took a drink. A sip, really. Not my usual open-throat gulp.

Then, almost against my will, I found myself putting the can down.

The guy watched me curiously.

"You don't want it?" he asked.

"Nah, I don't think I'm going to drink tonight."

For him this was probably no big deal. For me it was the most incredible and unexpected thing I'd ever done. I had never turned down a drink at a party full of booze.

I walked around that party for the rest of the night in a state of barely suppressed astonishment.

I'd turned down a beer. It was a miracle!

Sadly, I didn't make it very easy for the miracle to repeat itself.

I went to more parties sober than when I was drinking. I went to bars on $1 draft night, I went to house parties and wing nights. I faithfully attended Gin and Tonic Tuesdays, wherein my housemates wore bathrobes and cowboy hats and swilled gin and tonic on the porch. I did everything I'd done before except drink. I told my housemates I was "taking a break" and they didn't ask any questions.

I was young, damn it. No way was I staying home or hanging out with the oldheads in recovery. I'd been sure that sobering up meant the end of all fun, and it was turning out to be true. There is probably nothing less fun in the world than going to bars and drinking parties when you are a sober alcoholic in early recovery. The events and atmosphere wore on me and rubbed raw my newly hatched sobriety. My mood continued to shade ominously from grey to black. No wonder I drank. Being me was a hideous nightmare. I was paranoid and awkward and horribly lonely.

In that frame of mind, I decided to go with my housemates on a road trip to Ann Arbor, Michigan, to attend a conference of student cooperatives. Our co-op rented a big bus, and even the lightweights who used to frown at my drinking transformed into extras from a beer commercial the minute we stepped aboard. It was a mobile party and I was trapped. The singing, the laughing, the drinking games. Sweet Mother of God, it all looked so much better than being sober.

I sat fuming as everyone around me got bombed.

"What's *your* problem?" asked a nursing student with permanently bad breath due to her overly restrictive diet. She'd been the most judgmental of all about my drinking, the most condemning. Which, in my mind, meant that she should *support* me now that I was trying to be sober! Couldn't she see that I was struggling here? I just couldn't win with these people.

Without waiting to hear what my problem was or why I looked like someone about to take a large bite of a rat's ass, she cried "Shot gun!" and proceeded to do a bad job of gulping down a beer in one long, slobbery, incompetent swallow.

Amateur, I fumed.

I was dying inside. All I wanted was to get loaded, to stop feeling vicious toward myself and everyone else. No one gave a shit. Even my closest friend, an older student teacher, wasn't helping. She knew I was trying to sober up and had been quite encouraging. But she was pounding them back along with everyone else.

I fought the inevitable. I won't drink, I told myself. I WILL NOT DRINK. I repeated this over and over until finally we hit Ann Arbor. There, we threw our belongings down in the basement of the co-op we were sleeping in and headed out to find dinner and go to the frat party we'd been told about.

I'd seen frats around Toronto and had always despised them and everything they stood for. Pastel-polo-shirt–wearing boys and girls who'd never known a moment of realness. I was offended at the notion that they had to create these annoying, artificial clubs to keep other people out. It goes without saying that I knew I was not and never had been frat or sorority material. This burned me deeply, despite my pretension of being above it.

The Victorian houses that lined frat row in Toronto were minor key compared to the places we saw in Ann Arbor. The Greeks in this university town were housed in imposing mansions fronted by rolling lawns lit up by massive floodlights. College kids, most of whom seemed to be clean-cut white boys wearing shorts despite the frigid Michigan weather, wandered everywhere. They were all, so far as I could tell in my fiending state, completely wasted. Every single person in America was fucked up. Except me. Which was unfortunate and ironic since getting fucked up was pretty much my only talent.

Everyone we encountered had a large plastic cup full of beer in his or her hand. God, how could I have been so wrong about frats? To think I could have been partying with these masters of the form for years now.

All at once, the combination of saturation exposure to drinking and insecurity about being a socialist co-oper in an ocean of wealthy, shorts-wearing, sports car–driving American preppies who had parties that involved hundreds of guests and dozens of beer kegs broke my resolve. I was going to get loaded. Really loaded. Just once more. I could sober up again when we got back to Toronto. I'd made it six weeks. That was enough. Tonight, I was going to party like it was 1989. Which, after all, it was.

My teacher friend and I went for something to eat before we entered the fray. Before parties, my eagerness to drink would make my stomach churn and I'd have to go to the bathroom ten times. This was worse. It was hard to breathe. Liz and I sat in the dumpy college bar with red vinyl booths and crumb-scattered table waiting for our food.

"Liz," I said, nearly panting from some obscure alcohol-anticipation-induced nervous system attack. "I think I'm going to, you know."

She stared at me, uncomprehending.

"I'm going to drink tonight."

She looked stricken.

"Why?" she asked. "You were doing so well."

I'd thought she'd be happy about my decision. I'd always been pleased when any friend who'd been dumb enough to quit drinking started again.

"It's too hard," I told her. And I meant it. It was too hard to be twenty years old, surrounded by booze on every front, and not drink. Sobriety was too hard. Being trapped in my head was a nightmare.

"We can go back to the house and take it easy," she said. Was she pleading with me? This wasn't what I'd had in mind at all. Even the drinkers didn't want me back.

"I'm fine. I'll just have a few tonight. I can quit again tomorrow."

We went back and forth a few times about how she didn't think I should drink, but I told her I'd made up my mind. It's too hard, was my refrain. Too hard. I can't do it. I won't do it. *I don't want to do it.*

Half an hour later we stood in the backyard of one of the enormous frat mansions in the long lineup inching toward the keg. My heart hurt from the Herculean effort to rationalize my decision. It was over. This sobriety thing was over. I'd made a brave and valiant effort, but staying sober was just too hard.

The line moved slowly. I could barely hear the top-forty music thumping over the blood sloshing in my ears as I tried to control my surging anticipation. I could almost feel the cool and wet of the plastic cup in my hand, taste the weak beer. Maybe someone would have some pills. Or a little blow. And beyond that, oblivion. A much-needed and relatively inexpensive holiday from myself.

The klieg lights could barely penetrate the inky black of the Michigan night. I was focused only on the keg.

Two giggling girls ahead of us, so young and normal-looking, so different outside than I felt inside, took their dripping cups of beer and disappeared into the crowd. We were up next. I stood with Liz, waiting to be handed a cup. I noticed they weren't carding. Good thing, because I wasn't old enough to drink in Michigan. The long weeks of grinding it out were about to end.

The guy working the keg whispered something to another guy, who climbed onto a crate and spoke into a bullhorn.

"Dudes," he brayed to the milling crowd. "Keg's dry! Party's over."

Around us a moan of disappointment went up, cheerful resignation, from all quarters. Except for me. I nearly went to my knees. It wasn't disappointment that drove me there. It was relief.

15

Self-Supporting through
Our Own Obsessions

TRUISMS ARE HEAPED ON by the bucketful in recovery programs. It's tempting to ignore them. That's what I did with the ones I found inconvenient. For instance, it was suggested to me that alcoholics and addicts have a habit of swapping addictions when they first sober or clean up and I should be alert to that possibility. I scoffed at the prospect. No way was I going to escape from a drinking problem only to veer directly into the path of an eating disorder, compulsive gambling habit, or raging desire to have sex with inappropriate people. That shit was just sick.

I took what I considered the responsible approach. Since hanging out in drinking situations had gotten too uncomfortable and spending too much time alone with my thoughts was worse, I took up the mantle of hard work, referred to in certain humourless circles as workaholism. In addition to my gig at the yarn store, which kept me busy five days a week from nine until five, I decided to take a full-time job at a late-night dessert place in my neighbourhood.

I would return home after a long day of sitting at the counter at the yarn store trying to avoid customer questions, lie down for an hour, then get up and head to the dessert shop, or, as I came to think of it, Hell II.

At first the managers at Hell II tried to get me to wait tables. I'd waitered before, in a cabaret in Smithers in the year between barely graduating from high school and heading to college. For my "training shift" there I was given a cash float and sent out to do battle with the patrons. My grasp of basic math was shaky and even though they were mostly drunk, the clientele soon realized that I could be counted on to screw up everything from their drinks to their change. I specialized not in shortchanging them but in overpaying them. As a result, I always ended up owing the bar money at the end of the night. I worked at the club for two months and never received a paycheque because it all went to paying back what I owed. The only thing that redeemed the experience was one very slow night when a pair of young men came in. They'd spent the last several months isolated in a mining camp and were bushed and flush with cash—an excellent combination from a server's point of view. They decided to have a tipping contest and I was the lucky recipient. When the night was over I had three hundred and fifty dollars. It was the only money I made during my first waitering experience.

The managers at Delectable Desserts soon realized that table service was not my forte, so they taught me to make drinks: cappuccinos, lattes, and so on. It turned out that my churning nervous system, which went on high alert due to sleep deprivation at around ten, made me a highly effective barista. I could turn out perfect drinks faster than anyone they'd ever seen. This was because I was in a state of near panic for most of my shift. Christ! I'd scream internally as the orders piled up. I can't keep up! I'm going down!

I've always had a flair for learning certain rote tasks and that's what coffee making is. And I've always been a harsh worrier. Unless I'm well ahead, I feel behind.

Double D used to get busy at around eleven o'clock, and it stayed busy until three or four in the morning. That whole time

I frantically poured espressos and steamed foam as though the penalty for wasted motion was death. When the doors finally closed in the early morning hours, I'd be on the verge of collapse. My feet hurt, my head ached, and I reeked of coffee. The espresso beans I munched like popcorn throughout my shift didn't help.

But on the plus side, I didn't think about myself or drinking even once during my time at Desserts. I was pure worry in action.

I'd walk the eight blocks home with streaks of dawn light cracking through the smog, go to bed, and wake up at 8 a.m., put on my all-black outfit, and head to the yarn store. Before long, I was a mess. Almost as bad as I'd been when I was drinking. I felt hung over all the time as well as irritable. I wasn't eating properly. But I was also deeply invested in the idea that the people I met in recovery who didn't work were morally suspect. My ability to hold down two full-time jobs at once meant that I was different and probably quite a bit less screwed up than they were. Plus, there was the money. I was making myself secure! Work was something I could control, and I controlled it with a vengeance.

I came by my approach honestly. As noted, my brothers and I had been indoctrinated in the importance of work practically since infancy. I knew a lot of people for whom work was the only thing standing between them and oblivion.

The ten commandments of work, at least according to my mother:

1 You must have at least one job and preferably more by the time you are seventeen.
2 You must take pretty much any job you are offered, so long as it's not seriously against the law.

3 You must not ask how much you will be paid. To do so is rude. You'll find out when you get your first cheque.

4 It doesn't matter how much you are paid. What matters is that you work. At least two jobs.

5 It doesn't matter whether you are qualified for your work. You'll learn. Because work is the most important thing in the world.

6 Even if you are in danger of dying of a hangover, you should still go to work. Throwing up during your shift is what the employee bathrooms are for. (Naturally, we weren't breeding surgeons in our family. Also, I may have made this rule up.)

7 People who don't work are bad. They are unlikely to get into heaven.

8 Heaven is a place where everyone has good jobs. Lots of them.

9 Job satisfaction is not the key. Neither is job performance. The essential thing is having a job and going to it.

10 Retirement is a myth. When you finally quit your main job, then you are free to get all different kinds of jobs that are suitable for older people.

I was clear on all these rules, but more and more people at meetings were dropping hints about how I might be using work to avoid my feelings. I rejected that theory outright. The people who refused to get jobs so they could focus on their recoveries were the avoiders. I was the facer!

When people in meetings said that recovery had to come first, that anything I put in front of it would be taken away, I ignored them. At least until I couldn't any more.

I lasted about a month with the new schedule and then it all went to hell. First, perhaps due to my increasing spaciness and hollow-eyed, brain-numbed presence, the owner of the yarn store became convinced I was stealing from her. I wasn't, but there is no real way to prove you're not a thief once someone is convinced you are. Once accused, you will forever be the girl just waiting for her chance to steal from the till. Perhaps Calvin told her I was trying to stop drinking. It's possible that in her mind, which often seemed almost as fuzzy as the yarns she preferred, that meant I was an embezzler.

All I know is that it all came to a head one afternoon right before I was due to leave for the day.

My boss was flipping through the bills in the open cash register.

"There was a ten-dollar bill in here," she said.

I paid no attention. I was trying to decide how I was going to get home without passing out from exhaustion and heat stroke.

"Did someone take it?" she insisted.

Calvin said he hadn't seen it, and something in her voice finally got my attention.

I said I hadn't seen it either.

"Susan, are you sure you didn't see it? Because it was right there a few minutes ago."

I felt my face flush. I still had the habit of feeling guilty, no matter what I'd done.

"I didn't see it."

"Well, then I don't know where it went," she said, accusingly.

Calvin's eyes widened as he looked from me to the boss.

"All I know is that there was ten dollars there a few minutes ago and now it's gone."

I opened my purse and pulled out my wallet. "Look," I said, nearly yelling now. "There's nothing in here! I don't have it. I didn't take your stupid money."

She said nothing and I could tell she didn't believe me.

I patted myself down. I was wearing tights and a black T-shirt and slippers. No pockets.

"I don't have it!" I protested again.

"Hmmm," she replied.

Calvin gave me a sympathetic look, and I understood that my time at Yarn Inc. was over. I was falsely accused. I was shattered. But I was also fairly relieved. My career as a knitting impersonator ended.

When I'd been sober for ninety days, Calvin came to watch me take a chip at the meeting near my house. He clapped twice as long and as hard as everyone else and I was grateful for every minute I'd spent at that store.

A few weeks after that, I quit Delectable Desserts too. I was beginning to realize that I wasn't cut out for that much coffee consumption. Also I was worried that I might have a stroke if we had another very busy Friday night.

Still, I wasn't quite ready to give up compulsive work. After all, I prided myself on my ferocious new Calvinist work ethic. I immediately got a job managing a record store. Never mind that I'd never worked in a record store before. The guy doing the hiring clearly hated the corporation for which he worked (a chain with head offices in Montreal) and liked my new, thigh-high boots in equal measure. During my time at Yarn Inc. I'd turned myself into a mod and the look was exactly right for my new gig.

I loved being the manager of a record store. *This*, I would think with great satisfaction when I arrived extra early each morning, *is why I stopped drinking!* I wanted to lead a fulfilling life. I wanted to be cultural. It was hard to be cultural when you had a habit of falling down in the street and being unable to get up. Rule number one of being cultural: Be ambulatory!

The other best part about working for Frugal Records was telling people what I did.

"Me? Oh, I'm the manager of a record store."

I'd always aspired to be a music snob, but thanks to the brain damage I inflicted on myself with my drinking, I didn't have the memory for it. But my manager title made people assume I knew what I was talking about. I was less keen to tell people what music store I worked for. It would have been better to be employed by an independent, but one of them might have wanted me to be qualified.

Frugal Records was located on Bloor Street in the Annex. The neighbourhood was populated by students, academics, professionals, restaurant and bar staff, the homeless, and everyone in between. In other words, it was a downtown Toronto neighbourhood. A group of street kids liked to panhandle near the store. These latter-day punks were more punk than the seventies originals, if you judged by number of piercings, height of Mohawks, and numbers of rips per garment. This, I thought, is what it's all about. Authenticity! Real life! And I'm finally sober enough to appreciate it!

Some of them may have been representative of the hard-knocks life, but I'm also fairly sure some of them were suburban kids slumming it. They were objects of great wonder to me.

Frugal Records' head office used to fax us a play list every Monday. This was a list of records we were supposed to play. Quality was not factored into the decision. The first month I worked at Frugal Records we had to play Milli Vanilli, Cher, and a Doobie Brothers greatest hits album. Not exactly the hot list of an aspiring music snob. Our store was equipped with speakers that piped music out onto Bloor Street, which served to amplify the noise and my embarrassment considerably. The bands on the list didn't really go with my boots or with my new sober but cutting-edge and alternative lifestyle.

When the punks started to congregate outside the store, I tried to play music I thought they'd appreciate. The punks scared off paying customers, but I didn't want us to have the kind of customers who'd be scared of genuine street youth. I played The Replacements, which I had to buy somewhere else, Hüsker Dü, Jane's Addiction, and the Pixies. Whenever the punks said "Hi" to me, I was thrilled.

They started coming in asking me to play their tapes, which we definitely didn't carry. I blasted Dayglo Abortions and Dead Kennedys and that further served to keep the customers out in droves.

In fact, the only customers who weren't scared off were the ones who stole things. Interestingly, it wasn't the street kids who had the light fingers. It was older people, men and women in their thirties and forties. They came in with large canvas bags and would spend hours poring over the shelves. They never bought anything and it took me a long time to figure out they were ripping us off. News of the incompetent new manager at the Frugal Records on Bloor Street spread through the professional shoplifting community and soon I had lineups of shoplifters out the door.

As I cottoned on to the level of what my regional manager referred to as "shrinkage" in the store, I tried to stem the tide of CDs and cassettes going through the door but couldn't. I followed the thieves around, but they didn't care. As soon as I went to the counter or the bathroom, they'd shove things into their bags and leave. I didn't think I was allowed to ban them based solely on my suspicions. Didn't I have to catch them in the act? And even if I did catch one, what was I going to do about it? Tackle them? Confront them? I was not one for confrontation. At least not while I was sober.

My sober dream job was becoming increasingly stressful. It wasn't just problems with punks and thieves, I also had no idea how to manage my staff. I had two, who, like me, had also been hired by the previous management team. There was Helene, a French-Canadian girl who dressed like Pocahontas and had enormous breasts, unfettered by a bra, that she liked to rub against people. Then there was Nelson, a nineteen-year-old Ian Astbury look-alike who, I'd been told, was a good worker. He got over that as soon as I became the manager. My tall boots and severe bobbed haircut (so long, spiral perm!) were not enough to command my staff's respect. Like the shoplifters and the street kids, Nelson and Helene seemed to sense that I wasn't entirely confident in my managerial abilities and they took advantage. They would leave the store a mess, forget to deposit the money, and defy every request I made.

As a person who was newly sober and just learning to trust myself to meet even basic responsibilities, this was daunting and frustrating. How could I make people respect me? Why wouldn't anyone do my will? Didn't they know my fragile self-esteem was hanging on this job?

I decided to add another element to my repertoire of compulsive behaviour. I stopped eating. Not completely, but enough so that I dropped fifteen pounds in about three weeks, leaving me emaciated and pale. Food I could control, even if I couldn't keep my staff in line. The flirtation with anorexia was blown to hell when my student teacher friend came home from a trip to Europe.

"What the hell is wrong with you?" she demanded. "You look like shit!"

I thought I looked quite svelte.

"Your eyes are all black underneath and your skin is the pits. Are you eating?"

I shrugged. And started eating again. I was lucky that she was so direct and that it was not an ingrained behaviour with me because eating too much or too little food is a substitute addiction/obsession that bedevils huge numbers of newly sober addicts and alcoholics.

As time went on, the cash never balanced at the end of the day if either of my staff had touched it. Finally, I received a personal visit from the regional manager.

"Susan," she told me that afternoon. "I like you."

The regional manager was a blond woman with feathered hair and she wore a hip-length blue leather jacket.

"Good," I said. "Thanks."

"But they're starting to ask questions down at head office," she said. "The financials are a problem." She looked out the front window of the store where a group of seven or eight punks had set up camp with their dogs and "Help Me, I'm Homeless" signs.

"I'm not sure the store's going in the right direction," she said.

"I'm sorry. I've tried … I mean, I asked Nelson and Helene to be more careful when they cash out. I try to be here, but I'm already working twelve hours a day."

She nodded as I spoke.

"I know," she said. "Staff. It's never easy."

"And there's this one night. I have to, well, I have to go to a meeting. It's important." I decided that the situation called for radical honesty. That's what the recovery people were always talking about. Maybe it would work. Honesty would be a new approach for me.

"I'm in recovery. I have to go to my home group."

She leaned in and shook her head, saying, "That's great. Good for you. So young and you've already figured out you couldn't do it on your own. That's amazing. Just amazing."

My confession was not only warmly received. It inspired her to make her own confessions. Right there in the store, which at the time was only thinly populated with shoplifters.

She told me she'd been raped when she was a teenager. That she never got over it. She told me the "honchos" at head office were pushing her too hard. She was on the edge. She told me that we, as women, needed to stick together, to support each other. She told me not to worry that our cash was out every time I let Nelson or Helene close. She told me not to worry about the punks in the doorway or about the play list. She'd smooth things out with head office.

We exchanged a hug before she left and I felt renewed. The emotionally open, sober (but culturally alternative) life was the one for me. I was on the right track and making progress, even though being the manager of a chain record store wasn't as easy as I'd hoped.

The following week I came in to find the safe empty and Nelson and Helene both wearing new cowboy boots.

I checked the accounts book. No money had been deposited the night before. I ran to the front to confront my lying, stealing asshole staff.

"The money!" I yelled. "Did one of you deposit it?"

They shook their heads. Helene also shook her giant chest under her suede vest with the fringes.

"So where is it? Who's been in the safe?"

"Don't know," said Nelson, his long sheet of dyed black hair falling into his face until he brushed it off with a finger adorned with at least three silver rings.

Helene stared at me open-mouthed, her Indian princess braids accentuating the vacuous expression.

"I'm not kidding, you guys," I said, starting to come apart. "That's two days' receipts missing because you two forgot to make the deposit the night before, too."

Now both Nelson and Helene stared at me. I realized that they hated me and they didn't give a shit what I said.

I was so screwed.

Summoning all my courage, I called head office. In an effort to sound like a team player and successful branch manager, I played Doobie Brothers, who were on the approved playlist, loud enough for the person on the other end to hear.

"This is Susan, in Store 14. I need to speak with Denise. We have an issue here."

I was told that the regional manager would be with me that afternoon.

I tried to reassure myself that after Denise and I had had such an honest heart-to-heart about very private matters, she'd be on my side. She'd help me fire my mutinous staff and give me some tips on hiring better, more obedient people. But it wasn't Denise who walked through the door. It was a man in his forties. He had male pattern baldness and a team jacket advertising an NHL team.

"I'm Rick. The new regional manager," he told me.

"Where's Denise?"

"She had a total fucking crack-up last week. Right after she came back from her visit here. I don't know where she is. Not in her job any more, I can tell you that."

"Oh."

And soon Rick was interviewing me, then Nelson, and then Helene in the back room. When it was over, Nelson and

Helene had both pointed the finger at me and Rick believed them.

"I got no way to prove you took the money," he said. "But I hear you got a history with drugs and alcohol. And that's enough for me."

I was instructed to get my things and go. My services were no longer needed.

So ended my career in music store management and all the image enhancement that brought with it. Strangely, I walked out of Frugal Records as happy as I'd been in a long time. Having a job wasn't the most important thing! I was sober and unemployed and practically prancing in my tall boots. It turned out I didn't live or die by what other people thought of me. Who knew the people in the meetings would be so right!

1 6

Higher Power

ANOTHER THING I felt free to ignore at my first meetings were all those suggestions about staying out of relationships for the first year. I mean, get real! I figured that advice was probably meant for the old people. For a twenty-year-old, a year is a long time. Waiting a year to get into a relationship was not part of my recovery plan.

I've met other people who had similar reactions to the suggestion. Their response was to get into relationships as soon as possible. Some of those relationships worked out. Other ones, not so much. It's notable that the young people I know who did wait the recommended year (and such people are approximately as rare as Andean cats) seemed better prepared when they finally did get involved. They'd taken the time to focus on themselves and their recovery and hadn't been distracted by someone else. However, I wasn't about to allow the experience and suggestions of others to get in the way of what I wanted to do.

When I was about sixteen it had become evident, even to me, that I was a slave to alcohol and, to a lesser extent, drugs. Sure, getting loaded was fun sometimes and allowed me (at least for short increments) to be the person I wanted to be, but I knew that what looked like teen spirit in my teens was going to look like pathetic sot in my thirties. If there was one thing the beer commercials taught me, it was that hot girls didn't projectile-vomit into crowds, as well as out the windows of moving vehicles. I was eventually going to have to quit drinking and taking drugs, but not until I was ready, which meant not before I was about to settle down with a nice man.

I ended up in recovery ten years ahead of schedule. I was twenty but after a binge looked thirty and felt a hard-up fifty. I had no romantic prospects and was a disaster, spiritually, financially, emotionally, and physically. So much for my plan.

Then I decided that even if I was going to be forced into premature recovery, I could still start working on the fiancé thing ASAP. Being sober would allow me to have a new kind of relationship, one based on mutual admiration, respect, and shared interest rather than one based on the fact that we both liked to get loaded.

After my initial bad experiences with the barf guy and Hank, I'd had a few semi-serious boyfriends when I was in grades eleven and twelve and during the year when I was waiting to go off to college, also known as the "year of my perpetual blackout." I liked older guys who drank a lot and who didn't object to me doing so. They were good guys, but it wasn't like I wanted to be anyone's Number One. I was already in a committed relationship with beer and wine coolers and, on special occasions, Crown Royal and cocaine. Anyone I dated had to be prepared to take the back seat to those true loves. At parties, I was always telling my dates to "go ahead and leave without me" when they tried to suggest that 3 a.m. was late enough. The party was over when the booze and drugs were gone and not a minute before.

My relationships tended to be predictable. I would break up with my boyfriends because they cheated (I loved cheaters, for some reason) or because the relationship interfered with my drinking. Occasionally, some unhealthy part of my boyfriends would kick in and they'd try to reconcile with me. This, I thought, was how relationships worked. Men tried to get back together and sometimes I would agree and sometimes I wouldn't. The key thing is that I was always in charge and I always cared less than they did.

When my all-consuming reliance on work was embarrassingly removed multiple times, I decided it was time to find someone to take my mind off my troubles.

Unfortunately, this meant facing one of my biggest fears— dating sober. The only way I'd ever been able to start dating someone was to drink, heavily. I was usually as surprised as anyone else to find out I was in a new relationship because most of them started when I was in a blackout or at least not in a position to make informed decisions.

When people, young or old, talk about their fear of being bored in sobriety, what a lot of them mean is that they don't think they'll be able to date or have sex without using. When they talk about the excitement of going to clubs and the nightlife, they often mean the excitement of hooking up at the end of the night. Alcoholics and addicts are notoriously lonely, and sexual intimacy is a way to forget about that for at least a little while.

I didn't want to be sober and painfully single for the next fifty or sixty years, but I couldn't see how I could date without getting wasted. Also, the pool of eligible guys seemed so small. I knew that I couldn't safely go out with a guy who drank or did drugs, because I couldn't handle being around that life for any length of time. The next time I wound up in a lineup at a bar, they weren't going to run out of booze. Part of me knew if I got loaded again, I might never want to sober up.

That left who exactly in the fiancé candidate pile? One of the old guys in the church near my house? Fuck socks.

My depression was noticed by a woman who attended the meeting at the church.

"You know," she said, "you should check out a young people's meeting."

I looked at her. I'd been under the impression that I was the only young person trying to sober up in all of Toronto.

"It's held on Friday night. You might like it."

THE FIRST THING I noticed about people in the young people's meeting is that the people weren't all young. Which was a relief. But they were certainly younger than the people I'd seen so far. Most of them seemed to be in their mid- to late twenties. Also, they were in freakishly high spirits. I slunk into the room and looked around, noting the heads tossed back with raucous laughter, the high fives, the good-natured ribbing.

Several of the guys in the room, while not fiancé material, were not hideous either. Several of them smiled warmly at me. I was immensely reassured by this. I still had it!

As the meeting got started, I realized that these people were similar to the ones I'd already met. Some of them were drug addicts, some were alcoholic. There was a smattering of the eating disordered. But where the older people talked about destroying their marriages and losing their careers, these people talked about getting kicked out of school and college and about being sent to juvenile detention centres. They complained about angry parents rather than upset spouses.

The other major difference with the young people's meeting was that there was enough sexual energy floating around the room to power a Greek shipping magnate's yacht. It was really quite bracing.

When the meeting was over, a few of the guys came up to me

and introduced themselves. Our greetings were awkward, since I was pathologically shy, but I left elated.

Most treatment centres consider relationships in early recovery a virtual guarantee of relapse. People who get involved during treatment generally get asked to leave. If they hook up right after treatment, they may not be allowed to attend "alumni" or group meetings as a couple. Not long ago I was talking to my sponsor about how worried I was about a friend who got into a relationship days after he completed treatment. "Most of the people who don't get into relationships in the first year are the ones who can't," she told me flatly. Well, there is that. But the risk is very real, especially when both parties are new in recovery.

All I can say is that the short, electrically charged encounters at that young people's meeting were enough to keep me from slitting my wrists until the following week, when I got to go back.

The second young people's meeting gave me a chance to do a more in-depth analysis of the guys in the room. There were the perky cokeheads, the funny crack heads, the morose junkies who specialized in bitter, entertaining stories about morbid subjects. Then there were the beefy alcoholic former jocks. This was my new dating pool. Every single one of them looked good to me. They gave me a new lease on life. Sick, I know. It was bad enough that I was going to have to be sober while everyone else my age was going to clubs and getting loaded and living the life, but the thought that I had to be single while doing it was too much. I wanted to get sober, not join a nunnery.

Also, my basic insecurity about dating and social situations in general, combined with my new and rather shaky sober identity, made me feel completely untouchable to a regular guy. Who the hell was going to want to date an alcoholic twenty-year-old who'd been to the places and done the things I had? I hadn't even been *cool* about it. I hadn't been in a band or in prison or *anything*. It's one thing to clean up after wreaking some real damage and making an impression on the world. It's another thing entirely to do all the damage to yourself, pretty much, and glean nothing from it but a serious vitamin B deficiency, bad gums, poor self-esteem, and a collection of stories that centred mostly on gravel pit parties.

Who was going to want to go out with someone like me? No one normal, I was sure. Then I started going to the young people's meeting and I knew. Some of *these* guys would like to go out with someone like me.

I also got a clearer sense of why experienced people and experts worried about relationships in early recovery. I listened as a girl in her mid-twenties with a badly set broken nose spent several minutes detailing her hideously abusive childhood. She said she knew that "new people should avoid relationships for the first year" but didn't feel like that applied to her, since she'd been sober like almost eight months. Then she went on to say that she'd recently begun dating a sixty-year-old man she'd met in a meeting. "Too bad about the guy's wife," she said, with a shrug. "But he owns malls."

After she spoke, other people discussed the "thirteenth step," which was an imaginary step in which a person with a decent length of sobriety picks up a new person under the guise of helping. Sign me up! I thought. I wasn't into old men with malls, but a young one with a car would be good.

The third time I went to the young people's meeting, I made it my home group, which meant that I put my name and phone number on the group list. The following night, I got a call from one of the other members.

"Jerry" was a genuine preppy, the kind I'd only seen in movies. In grade eleven, I'd attempted to turn myself into a prep, based entirely on my love of the Sparks' "Eaten by the Monster of Love" on the *Valley Girl* soundtrack, as well as Depeche Mode's "Just Can't Get Enough." As a small-town, blue-collar, heavy-drinking high school girl, I'd missed the prepster mark in almost every way (I was poor, I had iffy taste, and my only home was the one in the country, which had a septic system and vinyl rather than clapboard siding), but I was still fascinated with preps. And here was a real one, in the flesh. Well, on the phone.

Jerry wasn't very old, maybe twenty-six or so, but he had large permanent bags under his eyes which made him look like he'd spent too much time hanging around with Jay McInerney, which he may have. He wore oversized, expensive-looking sweaters with white T-shirts poking out underneath. His large jeans were held up by interesting belts, and his hair was a combination of spiky and tousled. I'd gathered from his comments at meetings that he was in art school and was recovering from an addiction to cocaine as well as booze.

"Hey," he said into the phone. "This is Jerry. From the young people's group on Friday night."

I swallowed and tried not to hyperventilate. I could do this, I told myself. I could have a conversation with a strange but perfectly normal guy.

"Hi," I said, my voice shaking a bit. God, no wonder I drank. Talking while sober was awful.

"I hope you don't mind me calling."

"No," I said, attempting not to sound like I was strangling on my own trachea.

"So, you want to go out?"

If there'd been a stick in my mouth I'd have bitten it in half right about then. I was having a seizure.

I croaked out a yes and asked when. I was hoping he'd say in a week or two. That would give me time to get my breathing and heart rate under control. With any luck, I might stroke out and die and wouldn't have to go.

"How about now?"

"Now?"

It was 9:30 at night. Since I'd sobered up, I'd started going to bed early. That's because the waking hours were the hardest ones. It was early August and the night outside was hot and still. Getting out of bed, getting dressed, and going out to meet a strange preppy felt far odder and more unexpected than anything I'd done while drinking.

Jerry pulled up outside the house in an old blue Ford truck, the kind one of my old boyfriends from home might have driven. There were not a lot of old blue trucks on Toronto's streets, at least not ones driven by art students as ironic accessories.

I was four months into my sobriety and my new mod look had solidified. The hyper-neat was a good fit psychologically, as I was trying to get some control in my life. I wore only small black clothing and had cut my hair into a short, severe bob with startled-schoolgirl bangs. I wore only square-toed black shoes or the tall black boots. Elaborate fashion overhauls were something I noticed other young, newly sober people undertaking. One day someone would show up looking like a hippie. At the next meeting they were a rocker. It was like we were trying on identities to replace the ones we'd lost.

Jerry didn't open the door for me but watched me as I pulled myself into the passenger seat. I saw him stare at the boots. He smiled. He looked so complete to me. Self-possessed and finished somehow. Everyone I knew seemed half-finished. Especially me. Jerry drove us to Yonge Street and parked across the street from an enormous games arcade. We played video games for an hour and barely spoke. Then we browsed in a huge record store and after that went to an all-night café.

Jerry started talking. He'd been sober since he was nineteen. He'd gone to a very expensive prep school in the United States, where he'd begun doing cocaine, then selling to his classmates. He started failing his classes and then got caught dealing. Instead of being sent to jail, he was shipped off to a famous treatment centre. The first thing he'd done when he arrived was to demand that they uncover and fill the pool that was being used as the floor of a meeting room. His sense of entitlement seemed glamorous and unreasonable. I could tell from the way he laughed about it, he agreed.

While he was in treatment, his anorexic college girlfriend had been sent to treatment for her eating disorder. There she met an anorexic male model and the two had hooked up. Jerry informed me that he'd basically been depressed ever since.

I thought Jerry's story was the best I'd ever heard. That's what addiction and love should look like! So classy! Like a movie!

I felt unworthy in comparison and told him almost nothing about myself. There was no need to go babbling on about my embarrassing small-town past, my unfancy and incomplete education, and my homely, unvarnished alcoholism with a side order of minor drug addiction and workaholism.

Jerry and I went out a few times a week. In a city where many students lived piled up two or three to a room, Jerry lived by himself in a renovated two-bedroom apartment that his mother paid for.

It was just down the block from his art college. Sometimes I'd stay over at his place. I spent my time there feeling breathless at being in contact with so much good taste. He had very good dishes. High-thread-count sheets and handsome bedding. His furniture was new. He had none of the usual Escher, Munch, Monet, or Klimt student prints I saw in other students' rooms. In fact, he scorned university students and their tastes as naïve. His walls were hung with original art, some of it his. Works in progress leaned against walls and filled most of the guest room.

Around the time we started dating, although he made sure never to call it that, I'd pushed myself through a painful wall of fear to enroll myself in an English class at the University of Toronto. It was part of a program that allowed mature students who didn't have the proper prerequisites to take one class. If you got a good enough mark in the course, you'd be allowed to enroll in the regular program. In other words, my high school marks (dreadful) and my college performance (worse) would be forgiven and I could be a real university student. I was beyond excited to be in school again, especially at U of T.

One afternoon, Jerry dropped me off on campus for my class. Students swarmed all around us.

"God," he said. "Look at them."

I looked around and saw the students through his eyes. Most of them displayed no fashion sense to speak of (we were, after all, near the Engineering building). They wore jeans and backpacks. They looked preoccupied.

"Yeah," I said and gave a rueful laugh, pretending I was appalled by them, too, while all I wanted was to be one of them.

"See you," he said. I slammed the door and he drove away. He was not one to engage in PDAs. At least not yet.

I waited for him to begin to pursue me. In my experience, that's how romance worked. I had a dependency on alcohol and dated people who developed a dependency on me. In high school I'd become a minor legend for the cavalier way in which I treated some of my boyfriends. To my enemies, it was a sign that I was the most cold-hearted bitch to ever drink an Old Style. To my admirers … well, I didn't really have many of those.

But everything was upside down with Jerry. I was sober, and still painfully nervous around him, even though he was my boyfriend. Not that he ever used that word. But we spent a few nights a week together and were always together on weekends.

I was sure that if I remained aloof and never let him know that I had feelings for him, he'd come around. He'd wake up one day and realize that he couldn't live without me. And the balance of power would shift. That day would be a huge relief because somehow without my intending it, I'd become almost completely dependent on him.

Jerry the Preppy covered up all the holes that my drinking used to cover. His money, his looks, his style, his distant, emotionally unavailable companionship were all that stood between me and what I was beginning to realize was an impossibly black and yawning void of nothingness.

I followed Jerry the Preppy around like a small lost dog. No, make that a small lost dog with a bad case of osteoporosis. I felt like the slightest bump would break something deep inside me. My newly adopted mod style made me a decent accessory for an art student. With his assets, his long-term sobriety, and money and confidence, he was my human life preserver. Of course, I neglected to mention any of this to him.

He would ask me if I was okay.

"Of course," I'd say, like it was a strange question. That was a lie. I got less and less okay as Jerry showed no signs of developing any sort of lasting attachment, never mind dependency, on me. He kept asking what I planned to do when he was gone. He was nearly finished his degree and would soon be leaving school. I couldn't believe that his plans didn't include me. I clung to the idea that my aloof approach would pay off at the last moment. That he would succumb to my withholding strategy any moment. I spent all my time thinking about him and how I could finally get him to develop an unhealthy attachment to me.

One night we were sitting on his very nice couch, and I was listening to him complain about some of the disappointments he was experiencing as he prepared to graduate.

"My prof called it decorative," he said, staring mournfully at the large painting leaning against the wall in front of us.

I bit back my immediate response, which was to congratulate him. Decorative sounded good to me.

"Mmmm," I said. I'd been reading up on it and knew that artists needed a lot of nurturing. If you wanted to go out with artists you had to be prepared to listen, to support, to accommodate.

"They all sold though," he muttered.

Again, I stopped myself from saying how great that was. Obviously, the fact that his paintings had sold during the student show was a big blow. I just wasn't sure why.

"To corporations," he said. "That's what I painted. Art for corporate waiting rooms."

This was obviously connected to the decorative problem.

"Three grand each," he added.

I inhaled sharply. When I was working full time I made about eight hundred dollars a month. If co-op hadn't provided food, I would have starved.

He sighed deeply and put his arm around the back of the couch over my shoulders but not touching them.

"So are you going to be okay?" he asked again. It was the fourth or fifth time in as many days.

I gave him a smile meant to show that I was a supportive, nurturing, good-listening, non-dumb-question-asking girlfriend that any artist would be lucky to have. Definitely no way he was going anywhere.

"Listen," he said. "I'm going to take you to a meeting tonight. I want you to find a sponsor."

He'd been pushing the sponsor for a while now. I'd ignored him. Who needs a sponsor when you have a boyfriend? Now a financial sponsor I would have been open to. I could have used one of those. A spiritual sponsor, not so much.

We drove to a huge meeting in a part of Toronto I'd never been to before and, as was his way, Jerry melted away from me as soon as we walked though the front door. I realize now that our relationship was frowned upon by many, and he wasn't comfortable with his role as a thirteenth stepper. But at the time it felt like he was embarrassed by me.

I sat in the first empty seat I saw. I tried to look surreptitiously at the woman next to me and got the impression of nice clothes and careful grooming. Her hair was cut into a neat, light brown wedge, and she had full shiny lips.

"Hello, there," she said, turning and offering her well-manicured hand.

I said hello. That was enough. I didn't hear another thing during that meeting because I was thinking about how to ask her to be my sponsor. I would show Jerry. I was an independent young woman. I didn't need him organizing my recovery. That said, since I'd started dating Jerry, I hadn't really met anyone else. No women. No men. And certainly no potential sponsors.

When the meeting was over and people began to put their chairs away, I turned to the lady. She smelled nice. She was clean. She'd do.

"Ah, pardon me," I said.

She smiled. Her eyes sparkled blue behind round spectacles.

"I was just, ah, wondering. I need a, uh, sponsor. I guess. I was just wondering if you'd …"

Her face became grave and she pulled a small, prettily bound pad of paper out of her purse, flipped it open, wrote something down, and handed it to me.

"You call me," she said. "We'll talk."

I could see Jerry eyeing me from across the room. I ignored the mix of emotions that roiled in my stomach.

In the truck he asked about the woman. "Did you ask her?"

"Yeah."

"Did she say yes?"

I nodded.

"Good," said Jerry.

"HE'S GONE," I gasped into the phone.

"I'm sorry, darling, can you remind me of your name?" came the gentle voice.

"My name is Susan. I met you at a meeting last week."

"Of course. I remember. With the cute boots. Now what's wrong?"

"He's gone. He left."

"That's terrible ..." She hesitated. "Why don't you tell me what happened. And who he was."

So I did. I told this strange woman how I'd called Jerry, who had been my boyfriend, although he never called it that, for at least six months, and he'd said that he had to go and answer the door. He didn't call back. And because I was playing it cool in order to get him to love me, I waited until the following afternoon to call him again. But when I dialed I got a message saying that the number was no longer in service. I tried again, sure that I'd gotten mixed up. Same message. In a state of mounting panic, I'd called one of his friends.

I didn't want to ask if he knew where Jerry was, because that would have been *dependent* of me. He saved me by asking if I missed Jerry.

"Well," I said, unwilling to commit.

"Can you believe the fucking guy moved to Vermont? He's going to love it there," said Jerry's friend and fellow preppy.

I hung up, buckled over, and began hyperventilating.

Sweet Mother of God! He left me! Not just me. He left the whole damned country! It wasn't supposed to happen like this. What the hell kind of bullshit was this? I never got dumped when I was drinking!

I spent a good hour walking in circles, flapping my hands like a fledgling bird. Then I saw the small piece of note paper with the woman's name on it. The sponsor lady. I was supposed to call her. I couldn't for the life of me think of anyone else I could talk to. The only person I'd told anything even remotely personal to since I'd sobered up was Jerry, and now he was gone.

So I called her.

And she listened. And listened. And after I'd gotten most of the story out, she said, "Would you like to go for coffee?"

17

The Sponsor

I MET HER in a coffee shop near her apartment, which was located in an expensive area in downtown Toronto. Even though every nerve I had was vibrating from the shock of being abandoned by Jerry to my own inadequate devices, I noticed right away that she was a miracle of grooming. Every detail was perfect. Her lipstick was shiny precision, her skin alabaster, and I'd never seen an outfit—sweater and slacks—look sleeker and softer. In spite of her perfection, she somehow managed to exude warmth.

"Hello, darling," she said. "You look wonderful." She seemed to understand instinctively that the normal social cues weren't going to work with me. There would be no small talk, no idle chit-chat. She'd either have to guide the conversation or let it die a lingering death at the wobbly iron coffee shop table.

"Are you still looking for a sponsor?" she asked.

I nodded dumbly.

"And you'd still like me to be your sponsor?"

Another nod.

Then she laid out her personal guidelines for sponsorship. It was brilliantly clear and practical. She wanted me to know that I could talk to her and none of what I said would be repeated. She was there to support me with her own experience but wasn't a professional counsellor. If our relationship wasn't working for either of us, there would be no hard feelings. If I was unhappy, I should let her know right away.

In addition to being stunned generally, I was stunned at her ability to speak her mind and to be honest and direct. I'd never heard anything like it. I might have been able to function socially if this was how friends always communicated!

After she'd set out the guidelines, she proceeded to unsheathe her cigarettes. They were quite a bit classier than other cigarettes, as was her lighter, which was silver and highly polished. After she lit up, she carefully lined up the package and lighter on the table and breathed out a perfectly formed plume of smoke.

"So, why don't you tell me about yourself?" she said.

Those were the words I'd been waiting to hear all my life.

Out it poured. Jerry, my drinking life, my social life, my work, my drinking, my drinking. My barely functional sober life. My drinking. I went on for perhaps an hour, during which she made only a few noises, of sympathy mostly.

"Oh, you poor thing," she said. Or "That's awful." Her words were beyond soothing.

When I finally wound down, she asked if I'd like another coffee. When we'd each gotten one and had lit fresh cigarettes, she told me a bit about herself.

Her story was fascinating, the way that many alcoholics' are. She'd had a privileged childhood that included being chauffeured to and from school and live-in servants. This had been followed by a marriage to a much older, very distinguished man, and then a series of losses, both of money and of love, and a drinking problem that flared into a bonfire. She'd gone into recovery and had been sober for three years.

To me, this was astonishing. Three years was an eternity. I'd gone nearly ten months and was having trouble seeing how I was going to make it one more day. Life as a sober person seemed unsupportable. Unsustainable. Or it had until I dumped my entire life story on this remarkably gracious woman.

Walking home after our first coffee date, I was tired in a way I don't remember being before. I was unburdened. Whatever it was that I'd gotten out in our marathon get-to-know-me session had left me feeling exposed and mildly deranged, but I felt lighter, too.

From then on my new sponsor, Willa, took me on as her pet project. She introduced me to people. Invited me with her to dinner parties with her friends, who were sophisticated professional people in their forties. She talked to me about money. How she'd lost most of hers and how she'd begun to get it back. She answered my phone calls, and we went for walks and had coffee.

I was dependent on Willa but in a totally different way than I had been on Jerry. Leaning on him had destabilized me more. He was the wobbly crutch, always threatening to go out from under me. When the relationship collapsed, so did I. Willa helped me to feel sturdier and more confident that I would soon be walking on my own. When I despaired of things like ever finding any sober friends my own age, she pointed out that there is often a lag time between letting something go and something new filling up the void.

In the meantime, I was mesmerized by her.

First there was the fact she was so clean. Elite surgical units had barnyard standards next to Willa. Everything in Willa's studio apartment, which was on the fourteenth floor of an exclusive building, was white. Her white bed was made up to look like a couch. Her houseplants had been recently polished. As we chatted, Willa breezed around with a small white handkerchief, which she used to dust anything that caught her eye.

"I love it when things are just so," she said happily, flicking the kerchief at the lampshade.

So did I. Nothing in my room at the co-op was anywhere as clean as things were at Willa's, but sometimes when I woke up lately, I'd notice a satisfying orderliness to everything in my sight lines. The sun's rays filtering through the blinds and latticing my Peruvian patchwork quilt were brighter. The day outside seemed to beckon rather than threaten, as had been the case when I would wake up hung over and paralyzed with thousand-pound remorse.

Willa knew her neatness was extreme. She told me she'd just recently begun using her wastebaskets. "Before that I would go downstairs to the Dumpster to get rid of things."

"You mean you took the elevator fourteen floors to the basement for every piece of garbage?"

"That's right," she said cheerfully. "But now I let the bin get one-quarter full before I take it down."

She took immense pleasure in eating and cooking and dressing well.

"Oh," she'd say before she served me something, "you are going to love this! It's so fabulous!"

Then she'd set down a white china plate of boneless chicken breast, four perfectly steamed spears of asparagus, and a spoonful of rice that held the shape of the serving implement. Sometimes the rice was from a package and then she would exclaim over how marvellous it was.

"This Rice-A-Roni is so wonderful!"

And it was.

From her beautifully blocked sweaters to her carefully applied lipstick, Willa was getting a huge kick out of her life. And she spread that enthusiasm to me.

Every time she saw me she'd say, "Oh my god, you look so adorable!" and then go on to praise my hair or makeup or some item of clothing.

I was, compared to Willa, a schlump, even though I was now a mod and tidier than ever before. But she seemed to see only what was working.

"We're the same, you and me," she'd say. "We get it."

I didn't know what "it" was, but I loved being in her club.

She took note of my various unhappinesses, mostly related to being broke and being lonely, and did her best to include me in her social life. But she also knew I needed friends my own age.

"Why don't you go to one of those dances," she said one afternoon as we were having coffee in Yorkville.

"Dances?"

"There are sober dances specifically for young people in recovery," she said. "I've heard people talk about them at meetings."

I'd always loved dancing. Like a lot of people with a substance abuse problem, I secretly thought myself an incredible dancer. Like if I'd just had some training, I would have put Madonna to shame. And when I got loaded, I became a maniac on the dance floor. One time when I was drunk dancing at a club that played only seventies stadium rock and R&B, I remember a man turning to me, looking me up and down, and admonishing, "Girl, shake it, don't break it."

WHEN THE FOLLOWING Saturday rolled around, I steeled myself to do this supposedly fun thing. I was going to a dance. Alone. Sober.

Willa called to encourage me before I stepped out the door.

"You can do this," she said, like I was preparing for major surgery or heading into battle.

I walked to the subway station to catch the train downtown. I thought about my situation. Nearly a year into my sobriety, I was still as afraid of new social situations as it was possible to be. Walking into a room full of strangers without any sort of buzz to drown out the fear was a prospect that made my knees shake. The idea of standing around in some church basement like the world's oldest, most socially bankrupt wallflower made my stomach hurt.

Would I be expected to dance alone?

Was I supposed to ask other people to dance?

I'd rather die.

I couldn't form a clear memory of school dances. If my friends and I went, it was only after we were so thoroughly loaded the events were a blur. I recall people slow-dancing while holding each other's asses at hockey dances, but those events didn't really count, seeing as they were more about the drinking than the dancing.

When I got off the subway, I slowly climbed the stairs to the street. The night smelled like heat and car exhaust. I fought the urge to go home and stay in my room until I was old enough to move into the retirement village for elderly, depressed, sober alcoholics and instead forced myself to walk into the dance, which was held in a basement just off Wellesley Street. I paid my six dollars and slunk inside, sure that this was the most pathetic thing I'd ever done. My whole life had been spent trying not to be as lame as I secretly knew I was. The entire point of my drinking was to hide my social and emotional retardation. And here I was showing up, friendless, and in a state of near panic, at a dance that looked exactly like the kind you'd see at a junior high school, only the people weren't as cute.

The huge dark room was lightly populated with people. Far too lightly. Quite a few loitered at the edge of a stage set up on the right-hand end of the gym. In the middle of the room, a knot of serious dancers were doing their thing. When I say serious, I mean they were good. They were doing actual moves above and beyond the drunken flail and the hammered hoedown. A couple of them were breakdancing. I slid up against the wall and watched.

The music was all techno and dance. C&C Music Factory exhorted everyone to dance now, and Deee-Lite said groove was in the heart. I'd recently begun to think of myself as alternative, because it seemed better than being a fucking loser, which is how I often felt. Alternative, to me, meant wearing black and listening to punk and indie bands and thrash metal. The Breeders, Nirvana, early Metallica, The Clash, and some hard-core, like DOA and Hüsker Dü. The makers of that music frequently seemed to feel like losers, too. No shame in it. I wasn't sure how the electronic dance music at the gym fit with my music-for-losers aesthetic, but it made me want to move.

I watched the dancers, and in a minute or so it dawned on me that I was no longer so scared. As my eyes adjusted to the dark, I could see people I vaguely recognized from the young people's meeting. Some of them seemed to be alone, too. The dim light took away my sense of being exposed, and I was about to sit down on the edge of the stage when a woman sidled up to me.

"Fuck, he's hot," she said. "I love his arms."

I'd seen her before at the young people's meeting. She was only a few years older than me, maybe in her mid-twenties, but she affected this odd, middle-aged matron style somewhere between Jackie O and Carol Burnett. Her hair was parted in the middle and flipped up at the ends. She wore a boxy, bright green suit jacket. I think she worked in a thrift store and it looked like she'd come straight there from her shift. She smelled like mothballs and cigarettes.

She was staring fiercely at a guy in a wife beater and baggy pants who was all pretzelled up and twirling around on the floor. He did have sinewy arms.

I nodded.

"And I fuckin' love this song," she said, starting to move her feet in a restless shuffle, still burning eyeholes of lust in the break dancer.

"Me too," I said, mostly to myself. I was having an out-of-body experience. I was at a social event *by myself* and I hadn't yet died. In fact, I was talking in a friendly, if meaningless, way with another person who was kind of interesting.

"Come on," said the girl, who told me her name was Rainey. I followed her onto the dance floor. She peeled off her green blazer and dumped her purse on top of it. I stood uncertainly, unsure whether to do the same.

She leaned in and shouted in my ear, "The place is full of drug addicts. Don't leave your purse alone."

Right.

I noticed her arms were scarred with ropy track marks and she noticed me noticing.

"See," she said, grinning. "Fucking addicts!"

I put my coat and purse beside hers. And we started to dance. Technotronic "Pump up the Jam." Soon we were surrounded by other dancers, most of them from the young people's meeting. A few of them were amazing dancers, the kind who showed up on boy-band videos. Others had more enthusiasm than skill.

After a few dances, sweat poured down my face and pooled at the waistband of my tights and, in the greatest miracle of all, my relentless thinking finally stopped. I had no idea it was possible to get a break from self-consciousness without putting yourself into a drug- and alcohol-induced blackout. It was a revelation right up there with that one-day-at-a-time concept. I wasn't self-conscious or afraid or ashamed or any of the other colours in my limited palette of painful emotional states. God save me, but I was free. Techno had done it! I was dancing in a hot, stuffy church basement, and for once in my life, I didn't care that I wasn't dancing with the coolest people in the coolest club.

After the music ended at 2 a.m., the people who were left went to an all-night pancake restaurant around the corner. Surrounded by club kids, cops, and hookers, we ate breakfast and drank coffee and talked in that slightly giddy way people do when they're sleep deprived.

I got home at around four in the morning. I crept into the house, trying not to wake up my housemates. As I climbed the old staircase, I caught a whiff of myself. I smelled like dried sweat, perfume, and pancake syrup. The guy in the room across from mine, who was working on a doctorate in political science, was on his way out of the bathroom.

"Holy shit," he said. "You were out late."

I nodded, trying to contain my enormous smile.

"What were you doing?"

I shrugged. "I was out with some people."

Oh yes, I was.

18

The Phobic Years

AFTER I REALIZED that I could have a social life and was capable of change, I started to love being sober. Not only that, I started to love being alive. I made friends with all sorts of people in and out of recovery. Many of the people in recovery turned out to be fascinating: the sheer variety of them was startling. And the stories they told! I dated interesting people. Enjoyed school and did well. I woke up *happy*. The craving for alcohol and escape eased almost completely the longer I was sober. It was therefore a shock, when the fear snagged me. I'd been sober almost two years when it really took hold. I'd always been a nervous person, but when I first sobered up, anger had surrounded me like an electric field and kept the fear mostly hidden. When the anger faded, excitement at my new life kept me busy. But somewhere along the line, I realized that I had inside me a Grand Canyon of emptiness that anxiety rushed in to fill.

There's a line in AA's Big Book that says that at their core, alcoholics are abnormally fearful people. I thought that couldn't be true of me, since as far as I could tell, I had no core. When I looked deep inside I discovered … nothing. There was a void where my sense of self was supposed to be. My strongly held opinions turned out to be suspect, even to me. My belief system was reduced to the conviction that I couldn't safely drink and probably wasn't going to win any awards for small talk. I'd never even been able to get a handle on how I wanted to look. It changed every few months. Now I was a mod, next a hippie, followed by a sporty phase. After I'd been sober a couple of years it dawned on me that I was acutely empty, which is about as lonely and uncomfortable as it sounds.

I was also beginning to notice other newly sober people who were shrinking away from life. Jesus, I thought. Why bother to get sober if you're just going to hide? Many of the clean and sober people I knew were taking bucketloads of antidepressants and anti-anxiety pills. They had trouble working. They had trouble living. So, increasingly, did I.

By this time, I'd left the University of Toronto, moved back to British Columbia, and enrolled at the University of British Columbia to complete my degree. The idea was to be a bit closer to my family, and I was leaving a fun but not terribly functional relationship. When the school year began, I started to experience knifing pains in my stomach that forced me to double over. This happened several times a day, prompting me to become convinced that I was dying.

I began buckling over in class, on the bus, and while getting ready for school in the morning. Frequently, I'd give a cry of pain to really increase the effect. I was sure that some former roommate had given me malaria or a tropical stomach virus. (As a fear-based person, I did not approve of international travel.)

Then I was pressured by my roommate into quitting smoking. He was a non-smoking friend from Toronto, and he, quite understandably, didn't love living in a tiny Kitsilano apartment with me and my pack-and-a-half-a-day habit. Soon I was buckling over from stomach pains while in bed, where I'd been laid low by nicotine withdrawal. The final chemical veil between me and the world was gone, and I was left with my random, catastrophic stomach pains and my bone-deep exhaustion caused by not having my smokes. I wasn't waking up happy any more. I was barely waking up at all. But I couldn't stay in bed twenty-four hours a day, no matter how much I wanted to, so I got up to drag myself to school. When the school year ended, I dragged myself around to all the hotels and restaurants in town, dropping off resumés, until I got a serving job at a hotel on Robson Street run by the world's fussiest general manager.

The dining room was overblown: studded with pillars that held up nothing; enormous vases of ferns and orchids. The tables were laden with so many pieces of cutlery that the oversized plates of overpriced food barely fit. Even the club sandwich was pretentious. It was topped with a towering contraption of toothpick, pickles, and olives. The wait staff uniforms were made of the same ostensibly posh polyester as the table linens, a sort of striving hooker's loose interpretation of Versailles-worthy fabric. I had trouble breathing in the restaurant, partly because the many managers running around the place with panic-stricken expressions sucked out much of the available air.

I'd waitered before, as noted, but never in a uniform and never in a place that charged twenty dollars for a continental breakfast. To make matters worse, I'd gotten a large tattoo on my ankle soon before I left Toronto. After not enough careful consideration, I'd chosen a hummingbird image I found in a popular book of West Coast native art. The tattoo extended well up my calf, and when asked, I told people that it was meant to signify not only that I was from B.C. (and apparently was not afraid to engage in a little cultural and artistic appropriation) but also that I planned never to have a job at which I couldn't have a tattoo. Unfortunately, when

I was fitted for my uniform, I was informed that I was required to wear nude pantyhose with my tablecloth skirt and matching tablecloth vest. And under no circumstances could I show any ink at work. The woman in the housekeeping department pointed at my ankle and said, "Don't let the general manager see that or you'll never make it through the probation period."

I was broke and so incapacitated by mysterious stomach pains and post-smoking exhaustion that I couldn't even contemplate trying to find another job. Besides, the hotel paid union wages plus tips. So much for my convictions.

I went to a store that catered to theatrical types, including exotic dancers, and got some tattoo cover-up. Before my first day, I worked out a camouflage. It took three thick layers of cover-up topped with two pairs of nylons to achieve full disguise.

At 5:30 a.m. I cycled my way across the Burrard Bridge in the grey dawn light to my first shift. My heart was beating far more rapidly than my speed warranted. I was having a lot of trouble catching my breath. I wrote it off to first-day nerves.

The job was, like a lot of restaurant jobs, stressful. We were expected to practically wrench dirty cutlery away from diners before it hit the table, and coffee refills were to happen at five-minute intervals. Our sections were large, and the table settings were fussy. Some of the chefs were moody. As the days went by, I got worse at the job, rather than better. My post-smoking lethargy had hardened into a suffocating blanket. I couldn't remember anything and had to write down even the most basic request. When I wasn't at work, I was asleep. On my days off, I would sleep for twenty hours at a stretch. On the morning bike ride to work, my heart continued to jackhammer in my chest, and I started contemplating ways I could manage to fall off the bridge. (Falling into traffic seemed a bit messier and more painful than taking an accidental swan dive.)

In addition to the terror of my job, of the restaurant-visiting public, and of restaurant managers and hotel chefs, I had managed to develop a crippling fear of flying, perhaps as a result of having been on the plane that later crashed. A week or ten days before I was due to fly anywhere, I would begin to have nightmares. The anxiety would mount as the hour drew closer. At the airport before a flight, I panted like an overheated dog and went to the bathroom every few minutes. On the airplane, I spent the flight in a state of barely controlled hypervigilance. Every noise was cause for concern. I stared at my fellow passengers, especially those who looked like they flew a lot. Did they look nervous? Did the flight attendants look concerned? Were they covering up the terrible truth that we were flying on one engine and about to run out of gas? What was that noise!?

I flew mostly to Smithers and back. I would get off the plane exhausted and wrung out. Gratitude at having survived made me exuberant for the first day, or the first two days. Then the sickening realization that I was going to have to fly home descended, and I would spend the last five days of my visit tossing and turning.

Soon I decided that I couldn't fly any more. It was just too hard.

I was also pretty sure it was time to quit working. Maybe I could go on disability? I certainly felt disabled.

I had been sober then for about two and a half years, and I was getting less functional, not more. I still preferred being sober to being drunk, but it was no picnic with fresh bread and good cheese, either.

Instead of giving in to the fear, I did what Willa had always told me to do. She was all in favour of getting professional help.

So I went to my doctor to talk about how tired I was and to ask for a referral to a shrink. I'd gone to a psychiatrist in Toronto for several months and found it helpful. Obviously it was time to see someone else.

My doctor, one of those dynamic young women fresh out of medical school, who later went on to work for Médecins Sans Frontières, took one look at me and started asking questions.

"Are you sleeping a lot?" she asked.

"Are you gaining weight?"

"Are you having trouble with your memory?"

It turned out I had something called Hashimoto's, a condition in which the thyroid gland gets knocked out by a virus. The lack of thyroid function causes exhaustion and mental sluggishness. Had I continued untreated, I would have gone on to develop a goitre on my neck and various other symptoms that wouldn't have done anything to make me employee of the month. Luckily, all I needed was a small pill once a day and those symptoms went away. I no longer had to make a note of it when someone wanted a glass of water.

Then my doctor gave me a referral to a phobia clinic at the University of B.C. There I underwent treatment for my fear of flying. Slowly but surely, the treatment, which consisted of desensitization, behaviour modification, and relaxation and information about aviation, worked. I could fly!

It's something of a minor miracle that my doctor didn't just load me up on antidepressants and anti-anxiety agents. It's a major miracle that the psychiatrist I saw before her didn't do that either. By actually fixing the problems beneath my symptoms, the doctors forced me to get through them. It goes without saying that this wouldn't have been possible if I were still drinking.

I've thought a lot about how I started to accumulate fears. They were probably there before I started to drink and do drugs. The other thing is that once I sobered up and actually started to love being sober, I became terrified about the prospect of dying. I was so in love with life, at least certain parts of it, that anything that seemed to threaten my existence (like my job waitering in a hotel while disguised as table linen) put my body and mind into a panic. I had no experience of working through anxiety but I had plenty of experience with using drugs and alcohol to avoid it. Left untreated, I could easily have become one of those people who find it a chore just to leave the house. Facing my fears, admitting them to other people, and walking through them was one of the most excruciating things I've ever had to do. Spiritually, emotionally, and physically, it was also one of the best things I've ever done.

In the years since then, I've been afraid to drive, afraid to drive on freeways, afraid of public speaking, and afraid of wearing my bathing suit in public, but none of those fears has ever come close to the ones I experienced in my first couple of years. I'm still not keen to die, but as far as I'm concerned, that just means that I'm having a good life. Addiction, for me, was about a slow death. Recovery is a move in the exact opposite direction.

1 9

The Big Do-Over

THEY SAY IT TAKES seven years to change every cell in your body. Don't ask me who "they" are. I'm just telling you what I heard. If that's the case, then it makes a certain amount of sense that I had been sober for seven years before I was ready to try writing stories again. I'd completed a degree in English Lit and was working at a publishing house. My last relationship with a creative type had collapsed under the weight of its own inappropriateness.

Perhaps I had to switch out every cell in order to flush the damage done to my imagination or perhaps I had to have a complete cellular change in order to be strong enough to face the rigours of the writing and, god save me, the publishing, life. As soon as I sobered up, I seemed to make it a firm policy (though an unconscious one) to date only sober or straight-edge musicians or artists. Obviously, I was drawn to the idea of creating something but not willing to take the plunge myself. I spent most of my twenties fretting over my boyfriends' artistic processes: Is Andre getting enough time to think? Does the smell of oranges interfere with Juan's ability to access his emotions when he plays "Hallelujah"? And I accommodated myself to their moods. Again, it was easier than picking up a pen. Until it wasn't.

One day I flipped open a boyfriend's copy of Julia Cameron's *The Artist's Way* and read about the daily pages. These are daily stream-of-consciousness exercises intended to help the writer free his or her imagination and get writing. They are also meant to help people make writing a part of their daily routine. The relationship with the boyfriend foundered, but I took the daily pages idea with me. I was working two jobs and had a busy social life and a lot of strange hobbies, so I felt I didn't have time to waste with writing that was just writing. I decided I should try to turn the pages into something, if I could.

Of course, I had to overcome my abhorrence of the blank page. As Margaret Laurence said, I had to make the torture of not writing worse than the torture of writing. This was not an easy task for someone who wasn't sure she had anything to say and who was embarrassed by nearly everything she put on paper. I decided that the key was to put myself in a position in which the alternative to writing was to be alone with my thoughts or, equally heinous, to have to stare at strangers.

Instead of my usual novel, I took a blank journal on the bus ride to work. Sure enough, I started writing. In fact, the first words I wrote in that journal ended up in what became, miracle of miracles, my first novel, *Alice, I Think*. It was as though the character had been waiting in my consciousness for me to listen to her. She'd been tapping softly and getting no answer until I sat down with that notebook.

Almost immediately, the writing I did on the bus ride to work became the highlight of my day. I reclaimed my driver's licence and bought a car and started driving in the early morning to an all-night coffee shop called Calhoun's on Broadway. There I continued Alice's adventures. The stories poured out of me, a collection of absurd, skin-crawlingly embarrassing episodes in a teenager's life.

I felt the same way about my writing as I did my sobriety—secretive, a bit tentative, both of which were balanced out by a surprising sense of satisfaction. It was another private revolution. When the book was done, and I shyly presented it to publishers, it was rejected for being "too raw" by many children's book publishers and as "too immature" by many publishers for adults. Finally, in 2000, I found a press willing to take a chance on it. That was a very great day indeed. The book went on to be published in several countries and was turned into a television series. But when I look back on that book and the ones that follow it, the greatest thing of all is that writing has allowed me to reinhabit the years I lost to drinking. I have literally rewritten my adolescence. Several adolescences, in fact. I've written characters with integrity, I've created characters who are socially gifted (in a funny sort of way), and characters who are disciplined and principled. All I need now is to write about an adolescent who can touch her toes and do a back flip and all my dreams will have come true.

In sobriety, I've even had the chance to revisit my many squandered hobbies and passions, like horseback riding. I decided to write a book about two young dressage riders. One is a talented, hard-working, responsible young rider. The other is extremely wealthy, unfettered by parental supervision, and owner of a world-class dressage horse. Between them they pretty much fulfill every fantasy and regret I have about my riding life.

I discovered that I wasn't the only girl to give up riding for a combination of romance, drugs, and alcohol. Since I sobered up, I've met several other young women who were "into horses" before their addictions knocked them out of the saddle. It makes a certain amount of sense. Horses and substances both offer thrills, escape from the real world, and that elusive feeling of closeness. Both can kill or maim you. Both require the sort of focus that shuts out everything else. If you want to work with a horse, you'd better keep your attention on it. If you're going to be an alcoholic or an addict, there's no halfway about that, either.

A few years ago I got to know a girl who at first kept herself hidden inside a tightly drawn hoodie. Over the course of a few months, she slowly emerged. Her skin gained some colour, and the sores on her face healed. When her eyes came alive again, she was extraordinary. Like a lot of addicts, her stylishness emerged only after she cleaned up. We went for coffee and walks and she told me that show jumping had been her great passion. She'd been good at it, too, going almost as far in the sport as a person her age could. Then she discovered partying and graduated from blackout drinking to using crystal meth. The barns she rode at were wild. Cocaine use was rampant among the people working at them, and she and some of her fellow young riders were trailering horses to faraway shows, smoking crystal the whole way. The thought of those young girls on the road, towing ten thousand pounds of horses and steel, was not a comforting one. When I met her she was in treatment. By the time she left town, nearly a year later, she was a different person. Like me, she regretted the loss of riding and horses as much as anything her addiction had taken from her. We talked about her "getting back into it." If she stays clean, I believe she will.

I did. Get back into it, I mean. As I was working on the book about the young dressage riders, my first novel was adapted into a television series, and I received a handsome payout, which I promptly spent on a horse and lessons. Once again, the best part, other than the joy of owning a horse, was the chance to redo a part of my life about which I felt such regret. My new horse, Tango, was magnificent and a heartbreaker, and in the few years I owned him before he died, I gained a full and explicit understanding of how much it had cost my mother in both work and money and emotional commitment to maintain a horse. The more I think about it, the more surprised I am that my mother didn't kill me at that fall fair.

I'm not suggesting that everyone who sobers up will become a writer (or would want to!) or an actor or a rock star or even get a pony. I am saying that those who stay sober for the long term often get a chance to redeem themselves in the areas they've truly messed up.

Take my squandered friendship with Giselle, my first best friend, for example. A while ago I got together with her sisters Christina and Denise for dinner and I told them how bad my memory was. They tried to stimulate recollections of our childhood together with a photo album. I saw pictures of us playing dress-up and stick and rope and belching in harmony to the soundtrack of *The Sound of Music* and some of it started to come back to me.

The flip side of not remembering the good times is that, as noted, I don't always remember the bad very clearly either. Sometimes it feels as though my poor memory is a tactfully dark blanket pulled over the corpse of my unappetizing past. I still don't remember the exact moment Giselle and I stopped spending time together. It was around the time my escapism started to be accomplished through chemical rather than imaginative means. It was around the time the games in my life became far more serious.

"Don't you remember the rabbit funeral?" Christina and Denise asked at our dinner. The proffered photo showed the four of us, in all our stick-thighed, straight-haired, tomboy glory, bowing our heads and pinching the bridges of our noses, paying our respects to four Old Style beer cases that served as coffins for the bodies of four black and white spotted rabbits.

"What happened to the rabbits?" I asked.

"The bear got them. It was our fault: We left them out in the hutch all night."

Several years before, when Giselle was sick the last time, we played Remember When at the hospital as though our lives depended on it. Friends and family tag-teamed memories, trying to surround her and protect her with a comforter of childhood recollections. I felt disjointed, not sure of my place. I'd been sober for nearly ten years at the time and was still coming to terms with who I used to be. When my turn came to stand over Giselle's bed, I tried to talk about the old times we had shared. But I felt like I had almost nothing to offer. I'd only recently come back into Giselle's life, and so much of what she'd gone through in the years between middle school and her illness was a mystery to me.

On the second to last night, Giselle's mom and I stayed with her. Giselle's mother used to call me her fourth daughter, and she didn't seem to hold my defection against me. Together we washed Giselle and massaged her feet. Freaked out by my old friend's pain and my fear, I tried a New Age patter, hoping she could still hear me through the red rush of the morphine: "You are in a green field. The sky is blue ..." But I couldn't remember the goddamn meditation. Then it came to me. That other game we used to play. "You are in the green field. A gentle breeze is blowing. You are dancing the Hungarian Bulgarian Goodguy dance to that song with all the jungle noises on the *Mellow Moments* eight-track. You are wearing your most hideous brown-and-orange-striped leotard. *You are winning the Hungarian Bulgarian Goodguy Dance Competition!*"

Giselle made a low noise, laughter slipping out from under the pain. "That is so shut," she whispered, remembering. Being with her at the end didn't make up for my long absence, but at least I was present and I will never forget.

The redemption process that people in recovery go through is slow and sometimes painful, but it's often as powerful as the dawning of the sun, and it's a process I see happening all around me. I'm certainly not the most dramatic or shining example of sobriety. I was not the most desperate case; nor have I become the greatest success. In fact, I believe that my story, in all its pathetic ordinariness, is a fairly typical example of the type of changes that recovery can bring. I've offered it here in the hope that other young people (and not-so-young people), mired in the seeming hopelessness and helplessness of addiction, might in some way identify and come to believe as I do that within us all is the possibility of profound change and the chance for an epic redo or, at least, the chance to be present for life.

20

Twenty Years and Counting

I HAVE BEEN clean and sober now for twenty years. I've stayed sober through an undergraduate and postgraduate degree, through career highs and severe financial lows, breakups with boyfriends and a wedding to my fabulous husband, through the illnesses, and in some cases deaths, of people I love. When Willa told me that anything was possible in recovery, I doubted her; I no longer do. It's true that in sobriety I've experienced my share of fear, anger, discontent, destitution, and loneliness, but in persevering through each new "slough of despond," I've discovered on the other side amazing compensating rewards: less fear, less obsession, more peace—the possibility of creativity. As a good friend of mine likes to say, I'm having a life.

The years, of course, have wrought other, even more inevitable changes. My status as a bright young thing in recovery is a thing of the past. I'm long in years, if not in wisdom, something that was brought home to me when one of my hip-hop–generation newly sober friends recently stopped by our house to visit. I was making potato salad and listening to music. She pitched in to help, and when a song by 50 Cent came on, she was clearly charmed. "Awww!" she said. "That's so cute that you listen to rap." Translation: "Isn't it a miracle that a person as old as you can hear music at all!"

But it got me thinking. If I've changed so much over twenty years, so has the world that my young sober friends face, and nowhere is this more apparent than in the rooms of recovery. When I sobered up at twenty, I stood out. Many applauded my decision to sober up early. They said I'd spared myself, my unfertilized children, and my as yet theoretical husband years of misery. Well, I thought modestly, it's the least I can do for them. Today the offices of addiction counsellors, and the rooms of AA and NA, recovery programs, and treatment centres are packed with people in their late teens and early twenties. It's the older folk who stand out in the crowd of the newly sober. With the advent of harsher drugs, for a lot of younger addicts, it's clean up or die. Many don't make it to their twenties.

I asked Neal Berger, an addictions specialist, what changes he'd seen in the demographic of people coming into treatment centres. He told me that at Hazelden, perhaps the most famous recovery centre in the world, the typical patient in the mid-1980s was male, was fifty-three years old, and had started drinking when he was eighteen. This typical patient was seventy to eighty percent along in the disease process. It had taken him thirty years to reach bottom, or the point at which he reached out for help.

In the 1990s, the typical patient was still male, average age thirty-six. This patient had started drinking and/or using substances at fifteen. He was taking a mixture of drugs and alcohol and was every bit as sick as the fifty-three-year-old man had been in the 1980s. In addition, this patient was often diagnosed with "co-morbidity" or mental illness, either caused by or combined with the addiction problem.

By the mid-2000s, the average patient coming into treatment was male or female, was under twenty-five, had started using at twelve or thirteen, was addicted to a panoply of substances, and also had symptoms of mental illness. This was a different patient from the one seen in the mid-eighties: this was a much, much sicker patient.

The trend is clear and ominous. Alcoholics and addicts today are much younger and have gone down harder and farther. Many, if not most, need professional help to have a fighting chance of survival.

In the light of this sobering news, I decided to supplement my own story with those of several people in various stages of recovery today. Interspersed with their stories are the observations of addiction professionals, as well as some general, if not wholly objective, assessments of the various programs available to young alcoholics and addicts today.

part III

AND THIS IS NOW

21

Swimming with No Arms

WE STARTED CALLING her Fluffy Sunshine almost right away. She was a small, voluptuous redhead who, no matter how hung over she was when she showed up at my house, always radiated a hectic but joyful energy. As we got to know her better, and her effect on the male of the species, someone started calling her Fluffy Pheremone.

After several months of struggling to sober up, torn between her obvious desire to change her life and the pull of alcoholism and drug addiction, she seemed to turn some kind of corner. She no longer had to report in meetings every couple of weeks that she was "coming back." Her occasional emotional hurricanes had moderated to the violence of tropical storms. After she'd been sober for a few months (in a row), I even began to understand what she was talking about, most of the time.

How this change? Well, Fluffy Sunshine got busy. She put herself right in the middle of a group of mostly older women. She volunteered for every job within her group. When she had been sober for a few months, she went to school to finish her high school diploma and started taking college courses to become a child and youth care worker. Little Fluff blossomed.

She's been sober now for a little over three years, and she kindly agreed to sit down and talk to me about where she comes from and what recovery from her addiction has been like for her.

She grew up in a home filled with drugs and notoriously bad-ass family members. Her cousins were drug dealers and her uncles were semi-famous for their violence. No one, she says, messed with her family. She remembers her mom smoking pot all day long and her stepfather being a drunk. A nice, slightly goofy drunk, but a drunk all the same.

She also remembers the parties that lasted all night. "You never knew what was going to happen at my house," she says. "Things could get pretty crazy."

By the time she was fourteen, she was a chronic pot smoker. She smoked at home with her mother and other family members. She remembers these family smoke-ups as some of the best times of her childhood. It was comforting to think that her mom cared enough to want to her to get high at home on weed that was safe.

The good times didn't last.

Her mother started drinking and quickly developed a serious problem. That left Fluff in charge of parenting her two younger brothers, a job for which she never really felt equipped. Her mother would disappear for days at a time. Sometimes Fluff didn't know where she would get the money to buy groceries. And then she had a bad acid trip.

"I was high for forty-eight hours," she said. "The trip was so bad it ruined my dope smoking. Every time I tried to smoke, I had a severe anxiety attack."

This was a problem because smoking pot was her primary coping mechanism. She smoked before school, at lunch, and all evening. She went to a doctor, who, at different times, put her on Clonazepam, Ativan, Paxil, and Celexa, all antidepressants and anti-anxiety medications. Soon she was taking the pills in combination. Finally she quit smoking weed and started drinking more.

Through all this chaos, Fluff maintained good grades. She took school seriously. She always had much older boyfriends and was popular. "I was definitely more of a leader than a follower," she said. "I had a good image in public and a bad one at home." By this she meant that she never brought her friends home because she never knew what condition her mom might be in.

Fluff maintained an epic party schedule. She got into all the good clubs and went to all the parties. She calls this her "selfish phase" because she wasn't around to take care of her brothers, who were getting into ever more serious trouble. By twelve, one was already doing "hard juvie time."

After she left school, she had no sober social contact at all. She would wake up in the afternoon and party until the next morning. Finally, when she was twenty, she'd had enough. She opted for what many in recovery call the geographical cure. She took the Greyhound across the country, drinking the whole way, and wound up on Vancouver Island. When she tried to leave her drinking and drugging lifestyle behind, she felt like a fish out of water. She discovered that she had no idea how to drink socially or to socialize without drinking. "How will I swim with no arms? How am I going to brush my teeth with no brush?"

She'd been to a recovery meeting when she was eighteen, but hadn't been ready. At twenty, she tried again. Every slip she had scared her more. She started smoking crack on her relapses, and the drug gave her the worst down she'd ever encountered.

But she kept trying. She called people. She went to meetings. She left a relationship she'd had with a much older, enabling boyfriend. And one day, it just clicked. That's not to say that life got easy for Fluff. She says she went through the stuff almost everyone does: transferring her addictions to food, clothes shopping, relationships.

But she was willing to try anything. Like many of us, she'd thought that quitting drinking and drugs would solve all her problems. "I thought it would be calm," she said. "But inside it's still a big shit show sometimes."

Her constant refrain as we spoke was that she's always wanted a good life, a better one than she'd had growing up. And her dreams are beginning to materialize. Those of us who've seen the changes in her over the last three years have marvelled at her intensity and drive. She's a Fluffy Sunshine Powerhouse. Like many who grow up in rough situations and come through it, she's got wisdom and a wonderfully dark sense of humour. I asked her if she has any advice for other people who are trying to get clean and sober.

"I had to realize that no one else was going to help me," she said. "No one was going to save me and no one was going to take care of me. I had to change my belief about myself. I had to change my negative thinking into positive thinking, and I had to put myself first. I had to choose not to be miserable."

Fluffy Sunshine Powerhouse. Future ruler of the world.

22

You Call This a Vacation?

WHEN I FIRST sobered up, I didn't have enough money to take a bus, much less go to a for-profit treatment centre. Nor did I like speaking to strangers, so asking a counsellor or social worker for a referral to a government-sponsored treatment centre was out of the question. Few of the other young people I met back then had been through treatment or rehab, either. Now it's standard.

So, in recent months, when a friend found himself in need of help for a serious drug and alcohol problem, I suggested that a trip to treatment might be a good start. The two of us sat in his dusty living room and checked out the websites of various treatment centres. Each site featured pictures of spa-like environs and employed the word "healing" on every page.

My friend gazed gloomily at pictures of ponds with fountains. "It would suck if the nicest holiday I ever had was to a treatment centre," he said. Like a lot of people with substance abuse issues, he'd had a very circumscribed life. It definitely didn't include any vacation destinations. He ended up going to a facility about an hour away from where I live, and on visiting day I got to see first-hand what sixteen thousand dollars for six weeks buys.

The Cedars is a treatment centre located in Cobble Hill on Vancouver Island. It looks like a cross between a meditation retreat centre and an exclusive summer camp. The architecture leans toward Japanese-influenced post and beam. There is a swell little yoga pod and miles of walking trails throughout the surrounding forest.

I pulled into the parking lot on Sunday afternoon and walked down a winding stone path and into the main lodge, where I joined a short lineup of mostly well-heeled, middle-aged people. We filed past a large table, where a staff person had us sign in and hand over gifts so they could be searched for contraband. It was a bit like visiting the most genteel of jails. The list of forbidden items included anything edible or mood altering, including but not limited to Almond Rocca and the board game Settlers of Catan, which I was asked to return to my car. In the room beyond, patients lay on leather sofas or stood, waiting awkwardly for their visitors.

My friend offered to show me around. He'd been in the centre for ten days and in that time had had no contact with the outside world. We visited the smoking area, clearly a central hub for most patients. If you've ever asked yourself where all the smokers have gone, treatment centre smoking areas may be the answer. Well, there and standing outside twelve-step meetings.

Even the smoking area had a faintly Japanese vibe. There was a sign posted forbidding men to outnumber women by more than one person and vice versa. I wondered about the origin of this rule. I had visions of multiple female smokers puffing away while a lone man was ravished by two other women, in the ferns at the edge of the lawn, just out of sight of the counsellors.

After our visit to the smoking area, my friend showed me the rest of the buildings and grounds, which really did feel very restful and healing. I began to resent that I hadn't gone to treatment. Imagine how well I'd be by now if I had! Fluffy Sunshine expressed the same sentiment. When I asked her how she felt about not going to treatment, she said she hadn't known much about it until she started going to meetings. She thought it was something only celebrities did. Then she went through a phase of being pissed off that no one had cared enough to send her. She said she still thinks treatment would be a good getaway.

As my friend and I sat at a cedar picnic table and basked in the weak winter sunshine, I had to agree with Fluff. The lawn underfoot was like a putting green. Around us small family groups visited and talked in murmurs. At exactly one-thirty, "the store," a small room off the cafeteria, opened and people began to converge on it. The store was stocked with recovery books, inspirational slogans written on rocks, candy, potato chips, and, most important, cigarettes.

We bought some chips and candy, then went to the cafeteria to eat them. Then we walked around some more. Soon, we were back in the smoking area.

After I got used to the overwhelming sense of peace and structure, another vibration began to penetrate my consciousness. The addict hum, one might call it. I overheard snippets of the conversations in a gender-balanced group in the lower smoking area.

"Yo, dude. So I like fucking nearly ODed G! Sold my shit to live large. Yo! Thug life forever." This was uttered by a young blond man who appeared to be approximately twelve years of age (though that was impossible because Cedars is an adult facility). He had on a baseball cap, worn sideways, and extremely roomy pants. He was apparently speaking to his mother, who looked tired.

When we went back to the TV room, we found a woman weeping disconsolately in front of a heavy-set man. I couldn't tell which of them was the patient.

Kids ran around while their tense parents talked in hushed whispers.

It occurred to me that inpatient treatment centres have to provide calm surroundings just to balance out the rampant and cresting emotions, the endless drama and intensity that follow any group of addicts and alcoholics wherever they go.

It's one thing to keep people's behaviour in check for an hour-long twelve-step meeting. It's entirely another to keep things from boiling over when dozens of newly sober addicts and alcoholics live together in a co-ed facility for six to eight weeks. Make no mistake about it. People in treatment centres, at least those in good treatment centres, are not on vacation.

There is very little "downtime." Rules are to be followed, and each day is filled with activities and assignments, including group therapy, exercise, and lectures. Many of the activities are emotionally demanding and designed to help the patients break through accumulated layers of denial about their addictions. That's about as fun as it sounds.

One of the things that treatment provides, in addition to one-on-one and group therapy and a highly structured environment that includes daily chores, assorted activities, proper food, and exercise, is insight into the science of addiction. I interviewed Neal Berger, the director of Cedars, and in a short space of time learned more about the science of addiction and recovery than I had in my previous nineteen years.

Like many people who sober up using the twelve steps, I didn't spend a lot of time researching alcoholism. I decided my best chance was to trust the program rather than argue with it and find excuses for why it wouldn't work. After all, the twelve steps had been effective for other people who were far more hard-core than me. Still, it was fascinating to learn, with the benefit of hindsight and my own experience, about how addiction and our understanding of it has changed.

Neal Berger has worked in treatment services since the seventies. His position as an in-demand addictions consultant takes him all over the world. He's also uniquely gifted at using plain language to explain complicated things like how brain processes are affected by addiction.

I asked him about the current prevalence of treatment and what effect it has had on the numbers and types of people in recovery.

Surprisingly, he feels that there was more and better treatment available in the late seventies and early eighties when the idea first gained hold that addiction was a disease and, as such, was treatable. During that period, there were many centres and they had decent success rates. Then insurance companies started to get ideas about how addicts and alcoholics should be handled, and unqualified people started to get in on the act, and the level of care, he feels, began to falter.

Still, most people who achieve long-term abstinence today undergo some sort of treatment, either as an inpatient or an outpatient, and just as the type of people going into treatment and their conditions have changed over time, so have treatment facilities. There are treatment centres that cater to celebrities and the very rich. These are wildly expensive and lean toward the "spa" end of the scale. Other treatment centres, such as the Betty Ford Center, are costly but relatively stark. There, clients stay in plain, dorm-style rooms and there is little of the pampering found in the more spa-like rehabs. There are bare-bones government-sponsored treatment centres in both the United States and Canada. In Canada, some treatment centres operate using a combination of government money and donations. Patients may be asked to pay part of their care (forty to fifty dollars per day and up). For those on assistance or with employment insurance, this amount may be subsidized by the government. While they are unlikely to be mistaken for summer camps or meditation retreat centres, subsidized treatment centres can be extremely effective. The average length of stay in government-sponsored centres is twenty-eight to sixty days, but some programs allow patients to stay for ninety days or even up to a year in some cases.

For-profit centres in Canada cost between $13,000 and $17,000 for a forty-five-day program. Costs go up the longer the patients are in treatment. In the United States, costs vary widely. Some of the best-known centres charge between $30,000 and $120,000 for thirty days. The expense of malpractice and liability insurance helps to explain why for-profit centres are more expensive in the United States, but the extra costs are also connected to the level of luxury and name-brand recognition.

The type of care and success rate between centres also varies widely and is not necessarily tied to the cost of the program. In the United States, there is a growing preference for evidence-based treatment. This is an attempt to introduce standard guidelines and measurements as well as desired outcomes. Evidence-based therapies may include pharmacotherapy to manage withdrawal and reduce cravings, and various therapies, such as psychosocial interventions, motivational interviews, behaviour modification and psychotherapy. Other treatment centres use a harm-reduction approach. This approach may not necessarily emphasize abstinence, but rather support a measurable reduction of harm to both the alcoholic/addict and society.

Whatever the approach of the individual residential or outpatient treatment program, the reality is that many more people need treatment than get it. By some estimates, only a quarter of the people who could benefit from treatment actually receive it. In the United States, state and federal governments spend more than $15 billion, and insurers spend over $5 billion, on substance abuse services for four million people. In Canada, most government-subsidized treatment programs and many for-profit ones have long wait lists.

The treatment centres with the best outcomes tend to be those with longer programs that include an aftercare component. Aftercare refers to ongoing meetings with other graduates and counsellors and, in some cases, halfway or extended-care houses that support patients as they start to work and re-enter society. I've met many people who've "graduated" from Cedars or Edgewood, a renowned treatment centre in Nanaimo, who've moved to town to stay near to each other and their treatment centre. It's obvious from watching them that these connections are important.

Some patients undergo voluntary monitoring, usually administered by the treatment centre. (Doctors, nurses, and airline pilots, among others, are required to do this.) These follow-up measures are combined, in most cases, with participation in a twelve-step program as the foundation of long-term recovery.

A final comment about treatment centres. Each has a different philosophy and approach. In the past, treatment centres were often based on a form of confrontational therapy in which addicts were "confronted" with their delusions. This can be extremely effective for some patients, but for others, among them those who grew up in abusive alcoholic homes, it can be risky.

It seems that children who grow up in such environments may suffer from a form of post-traumatic stress disorder. As George Vaillant, author of the groundbreaking study *A Natural History of Alcoholism*, observes, "Outside of residence in a concentration camp, there are very few sustained human experiences that make one the recipient of as much sadism as does being a close family member of an alcoholic."* This background may make children of alcoholics or addicts harder to treat than other patients. The defence mechanisms that help them get through their traumatic childhoods also allow them to tolerate extraordinary circumstances. Neal Berger refers to the most common of these coping mechanisms as "psychic numbing" and notes that children of alcoholics and addicts have a four times higher rate of relapse than other patients. The brain disconnect they engage when stressed makes it tough for them to grow emotionally, and these patients have to be handled carefully and made to feel safe. They might survive a confrontational program, because they've proven that they can get through anything. But they often won't get much out of it.

Memoirs about drug addiction and alcoholism are full of shocking, fascinating, and often entertaining stories about treatment programs. They are places where the high drama and low comedy of addiction take centre stage. They are also, sometimes, places where miracles happen. That said, those who are honest about treatment and the outcomes it can provide admit that it takes more than a good program, insightful staff, and scientific knowledge. It takes a willing and motivated patient as well as ongoing care and support. People who start out resistant to treatment may end up doing the best, while "treatment all stars," as Jerry Blackburn, the admissions director from Edgewood, calls them, may relapse as soon as they are released. No one yet knows how all the pieces come together. Somewhere along the

---

*George E. Vaillant, *The Natural History of Alcoholism Revisited.* Harvard University Press, page 22.

line, however, it seems that addicts and alcoholics must gain the humility and grace that allows them to give up their preconceived misgivings and to trust that somehow, their beaten hearts and minds can be healed.

23

Aftercare

ON A RAINY NIGHT in February, I met with a group of young people, most of whom were part of an aftercare program for Cedars. We met at the office of Sue Donaldson, who runs Pegasus Recovery Solutions in Victoria, B.C. She's a petite woman with short blond hair who exudes confidence and warmth. It's a mark of her personal charisma that she was able to get so many of her clients out on a Friday night.

The assembled group ranged from nineteen to thirty years old and had anywhere from two months' to two years' clean time from a variety of substances, including alcohol, cocaine, crack cocaine, and heroin. All had been to treatment at Cedars, except for a young man named Don who had gone to treatment in Maple Ridge.

The difference between the people with longer-term sobriety and those who were new was obvious. Nick, a muscular twenty-four-year-old who'd been clean for two years, chewed absently on his gold chain as he listened. He had sponsored at least two of the younger guys and was well-spoken and forthright in a way that was never overbearing. Abbie, a client who bore a startling resemblance to Rebecca DeMornay, worked part-time in a treatment centre. Her words also seemed to carry a lot of weight with the others.

We pushed back the comfortable furniture to accommodate

everyone. As I looked around at the group, I felt slightly inadequate, partly because the group was so young and healthy-looking. I introduced myself and my project and said I was trying to get a picture of young people in recovery and what, if anything, has changed since the late eighties.

First I asked if anyone had tried anything other than treatment to deal with their addictions. There were some mutterings about "willpower," spoken with the same sort of conviction a non-health-food person might use to say they took a few vitamins to deal with their advanced cancer.

Don, who had earlier volunteered that a few months before he'd been dealing crack out of the hotel located behind the office we were in, mentioned that he'd tried hypnosis to quit drugs. They all laughed. He said he was looking for a silver bullet. Several of the others had tried quitting on their own, but most had found it impossible and had resigned themselves to early deaths.

I asked about how familiar they had been with NA and AA before they went to treatment. Very few of them knew much, although all were now involved in one or both.

Reid, a twenty-one-year-old, mentioned that he'd gone to a couple of NA meetings and found them inspiring. "That one meeting ruined my using because I knew there was another way," he said. Even so, he wasn't able to stay clean and sober until he went to treatment. Most had been to see multiple alcohol and drug counsellors, starting in high school.

Kelli, a tiny woman with enormous blue eyes, said that when she was twenty-five she had been sent to meetings in Los Angeles by the courts, as part of a drug deferment on criminal charges. As soon as she figured out that there was no way to trace back the signatures she was supposed to collect to the people who gave them, because AA and NA are anonymous, she got her friends to sign her forms.

She was a heroin addict, and she talked about how she thought she'd never get clean and was sure she'd die an addict. It was only after she detoxed in treatment that she realized that she might actually have a chance. Kelli noted that her heroin use wasn't fun any more and that she spent her life just trying to get from high to high. She ended up in treatment in Canada as a way to avoid jail time in the United States for trafficking.

I asked how many of the rest of them had gone to meetings before entering treatment. A few had, but none had stayed. For some, the language of recovery was a barrier. For others, it was the age of the other participants.

Most of them had gone into treatment hoping only to quit their most destructive substance, generally cocaine or heroin, but they had planned to continue drinking and smoking weed. I remembered a similar plan for myself, only mine involved stopping drinking entirely and using drugs only on very special occasions.

As they spoke, the thing that stood out was their enthusiasm about recovery. I've seen the same thing in people I've sponsored. Once they finish detoxing, get into a program, acquire a few friends, and are no longer sick to death, they often become exhilarated. But their exuberance is usually tempered by some misgivings.

Kelli admitted to initially feeling ambivalent about the idea that she was a person "who has to go to a meeting to feel better" but said that she's over that now. All of them expressed an early fear of being "lame" or "uncool." In *Tweak*, Nic Sheff's heartbreaking memoir about his methamphetamine addiction, I was struck by this conversation between him and one of his drug buddies. He tells his friend he wants to get clean, and his friend replies, "You only get to live this life once. I'd rather be blissed out for a short time than fucking bored and miserable until I'm like ninety or something." Then he goes on, "This is life … this is living. Every day is an adventure." And Nic Sheff replies that it seems like every day is the same thing. He's grabbed hold of the truth there. Addiction is cyclical. The same thing happens over and over with poorer results. The group in the aftercare program seemed to have grasped that as well. The thing that convinced them to keep going to aftercare and self-help meetings was that they started to get better so quickly.

One of the great benefits of sobering up early is that most young people haven't had a chance to build much of a family or a career, so there's less wreckage to deal with. Plus, young bodies and minds are more resilient.

Two of the participants had spent some time in recovery while they were still in high school and both said they felt well accepted. This was in contrast to another young woman I interviewed. She was sixteen when she sobered up and characterized her last two years of high school as "hell." She got through it by hanging out with religious students, because they were more "open-minded" about someone who didn't drink.

The people in the aftercare group talked about connecting with their friends and having fun, like any young people, but all said that when they have real problems, they call the older people in recovery. Most of them had much older sponsors. Kelli talked about choosing the "old crabby English lady who sits in the corner" who had a habit of hanging up on her when she felt Kelli wasn't listening. They asked if I had a sponsor and I was relieved I could tell them I did.

When asked about their dreams during active addiction, several said they had given them up. "If you accept you have no future, it's easier to follow your addiction," said one. Annie, a pretty, pensive twenty-two-year-old, talked of her persistent fantasies about death, most of which involved taking acid and jumping off a building.

She'd sobered up in a treatment centre two years before and after treatment had gone home to a small town on Vancouver Island. There, she was by far the youngest person at meetings. The people were kind to her, but they weren't her peers. It was hard to change her old friends. And one of the things most treatment programs emphasize is that being in constant proximity with people who are drinking or using is one of the major factors in relapse. Dr. Steven Jaffe, an addictions specialist, writes that the most common pathway to relapse is "involvement with peers who use alcohol or drugs.... Spending time with using peers becomes too tempting and the [person] relapses."*

Annie finally moved to Victoria after hearing that there were lots of other young people in recovery there.

I asked the group about letting go of the darkness that surrounds most addicts and alcoholics, but the question was sufficiently vague that none of them seemed to know what I was talking about.

"You mean chaos?" one asked.

That they knew.

I asked them if they felt isolated in the non-recovery community and most said no. That they in fact felt more comfortable now.

At this point, Jessie, a twenty-four-year-old who'd been silent, spoke up. "I've just been keeping quiet over here, taking things in. But everything they said, about not feeling isolated, I feel the opposite." He went on to say that he'd gotten into a relationship in

---

*Katherine Ketcham and Nicholas Pace, *Teens Under the Influence*. Ballantine Books, page 303.

treatment. The relationship was "co-dependent" and he'd invested more in his girlfriend than in his recovery.

"These aftercare meetings are the only thing that saved me," he said. "I hated the other meetings." He talked about feeling judged because of the relationship.

Dale turned to him and said, very firmly, "So why'd you get into one if you were told not to?"

Jessie didn't respond. I gathered that the relationship was over, but he still seemed a little bruised.

I asked them if they struggled with substitute addictions and mentioned my experience of feeling like my addictive self was always casting around for somewhere to land.

They nodded and laughed. Dale talked about shopping, gambling, and working out obsessively. Annie called herself a "schoolaholic."

I asked if the educational component of treatment had been useful. In other words, did it help them to understand how their addictions had changed their brains. Most agreed that it was helpful. It took the "guilt away," said one. Don, who'd attended a different treatment centre, one that did not subscribe to the disease model but instead used harm reduction, objected to the idea that he had a disease. It was very clear from the discussion that followed that the recovery model employed by individual treatment centres had a profound influence on the way each viewed the root of his or her addiction.

Before we finished the meeting, I asked if any of them had anything they wanted to add. One said, "Tell people that recovery's cool." I made a note of it. A startlingly beautiful nineteen-year-old who'd come in late spoke about how several people in her workplace, including much older people, had started going to meetings because she'd told them about her recovery. Her face glowed. "I feel really good about that," she said. I thought that if I weren't already in recovery, I'd be inspired to consider it by the sheer joy in her face.

Then they were up and making plans to go out for dinner. I heard two of them discussing how they were going on a cruise with a bunch of other young people in recovery. One of the guys asked out one of the girls. She laughed. And so did I. I walked out of the building and made my way back along Douglas Street, the main drag into Victoria. As I walked past the knots of strung-out street kids, dealers, addicts, and drunks, I wished for each of them a bit of the light that I'd seen in the eyes of the young people I had just left.

24

Insane in the Brain

REMEMBER THOSE old public-service drug announcements featuring a brain and a fried egg? You know the ones: This is your brain, then the image of the egg being fried: This is your brain on drugs. Turns out those ads were fairly accurate, although our brains are likely being poached, soft boiled, or scrambled, depending on what substances we use to cook them.

Most addiction researchers have come around to the idea that addiction is, in part, a brain disease. This is something that twelve-step groups seem to have figured out by instinct and trial and error a long time ago. AA's second step—"[We] came to believe that a power greater than ourselves could restore us to sanity"—recognizes that the alcoholic or addict is not operating with optimal mental function, and brain scans of alcoholics and addicts do show significant changes to brain function and chemistry. Some people question whether addicts and alcoholics have altered brain patterns even *before* they start using. Either way, the brains of alcoholics and addicts operate differently from those of other people. HBO's documentary series and accompanying book *Addiction: Why Can't They Just Stop? New Knowledge, New Treatments, New Hope* do an excellent job of explaining and demonstrating the relationship between addiction and altered brain chemistry and function.

My friends and I used to joke about the thousands of brain cells we killed every time we got high or drank until we blacked out. It turns out we were doing more than just deleting brain cells. We were training our brains how to deal with life. This is one reason it is more difficult to treat people who start drinking and using at a young age and why people who come into recovery now are often sicker now than those thirty years ago.

To illustrate, Neal Berger posed the following scenario. A twelve-year-old girl is socially awkward, shy, all those things that go along with being a preteen. She's facing a stressful social situation, maybe the first day at a new school. She arrives at school, heart pounding. She passes a group of older kids, and one of them says something mean about her pants. The girl is so embarrassed and self-conscious she feels like running home and hiding. Instead of running home, the girl tells a friendly teacher or calls her mom or her older brother or a friend. That person reassures her that her pants look good and the older kids were being jerks and don't know nice pants when they see them. The girl feels better and gets through the rest of her day, secure in the knowledge that talking about her problems and reaching out to others will help when she's in trouble.

However, suppose that rather than calling someone, the girl heads behind the nearest convenience store and smokes a joint. Or goes into the school washroom and has a drink. What has she taught her brain then?

Both methods of dealing with stress achieve the same thing: relief. The brain perceives both talking over the problem and getting high as effective. But one method helps the girl to grow and feel more comfortable in the world, and the other one teaches her brain that relief can be found in substances. In her wonderful book *Drinking: A Love Story*, Caroline Knapp calls this the "mathematics of self-transformation … Discomfort + Drink = No Discomfort."

When I was being bullied in school or was simply uncomfortable in my own skin, the thought of calling my mother or any other adult never crossed my mind. Not once. By the time I finally took a drink to deal with my social discomfort, my brain was desperate for relief. For the next seven years, I put my brain pathways on a strenuous training program. When I got stressed—excited, happy, upset, or uncomfortable—I dealt with it by getting loaded. The drinking made my behaviour worse and served to isolate me from other forms of support. The chances of my reaching out to an adult or even a friend became much slimmer. I was, after all, a bad kid. I knew it, and I thought most of those around me knew it.

In recovery one hears people talk about how booze and drugs saved their lives, especially when they were younger. Then the substances stopped working and the cure became the disease.

The whole addictive experience may be connected to the phases of brain development. The brain goes through two main growth periods. The first lasts from birth to age five. The second occurs from age ten to twenty-one. This second phase of brain development is "an opportunity to grow more gray matter and, even more important, to organize the electrical and chemical brain circuitry that underlies maturity, self-control, emotional balance, rational decision-making, memory formation, social skills, intelligence, and personality."* But ironically, during this second stage of brain growth, from ages thirteen to eighteen, the brain is actually shrinking as it gets rid of unused pathways and makes the ones you do use more efficient. In other words, when we don't

---

* *Teens Under the Influence*, pages 42–43.

develop or make or use of healthy brain connections or patterns, they disappear.

Thus, you have trained your brain that drugs and alcohol are the best cure for dealing with discomfort, and it lets go of other possible pathways. You literally don't have other strategies available, at least so far as your brain is concerned. I can still remember how astonished I was to find out that talking about my issues with my sponsor and other people in recovery produced a quieter, but still powerful, feeling of release. Sharing, like drugs, is powerful.

This information made my behaviour and feelings after I first stopped drinking more understandable, but the onset of insanity when you're young is difficult to identify. It seems to merge into the whole teen experience. I was already self-conscious and shy. When I got drunk, those feelings went away. When I sobered up, they came back, worse than ever, requiring me to drink more. This last piece didn't register very well. I still saw drinking and taking drugs as the solution. I was lucky because, other than a phase when I was fourteen, during which I attempted to become a pothead, and later flings with cocaine and speed, I mostly stuck to alcohol. Younger people who use highly addictive hard drugs, such as meth and crack, do even more radical alterations to their brain chemistry. The stronger the drug, the more powerfully the brain remembers the effect.

Dopamine is central to this whole process. Dopamine is the chemical in the brain that makes us feel good. We get a little hit of dopamine when we eat something good, see something pretty, listen to music, or have sex. When we get drunk or high, our dopamine levels spike. After each spike, our dopamine levels fall, eventually to below the normal level. The following spike doesn't go quite as high as the one before it. Over time, the rush becomes smaller and the crash that follows becomes deeper. Most addicts and alcoholics have had the deeply disappointing experience of finding that the drink or the drug doesn't work any more. Often, this betrayal is the thing that precedes someone's entrance into recovery.

> Meanwhile, the brain has been fooled into "thinking" that achieving that high is equivalent to survival (even more so than with food or sex).... Eventually, the brain is forced to turn on a self-defense mechanism, reducing the production of dopamine altogether—and weakening the pleasure circuit's function. At this point, the addicted person is compelled to use the substance not to get high, but to feel "normal"—since there's little or no dopamine to be had. (*Addiction*, p. 59)

In other words, abusing drugs and alcohol destroys our ability to feel pleasure in everyday life when we are not high, which explains why early recovery can feel like such a brutal slog.

The good news is, the brain can be reprogrammed, if somewhat slowly. This lag time is something that the founders of twelve-step programs seem to have intuited. There's a line in the Big Book of Alcoholics Anonymous about "trudging the road of happy destiny." They used the word *trudging* as opposed to *skipping* or *prancing* because early sobriety is not for the faint of heart. The length of time it takes for brain damage inflicted by addiction to heal differs based on your early life and on what substances and what quantities of substances you were using. Most experts suggest that if you can make it six months without a relapse, your chances are greatly enhanced. If you can go two years, you are really on the road to long-term recovery. *That doesn't mean, however, you'll be able to use safely after two years.* It just means that much of the damage you've done to yourself that can be repaired will have been by then.

Why, then, do people go to self-help programs and stay in them, year after year? The reason is that twelve-step programs not only help to heal brain function, they provide social supports that are uniquely tailored to people in recovery. Programs based on the twelve steps and other types of support, such as counselling and behaviour modification, help people to learn to delay gratification (addicts and alcoholics are notoriously impatient for a quick fix) and to deal with the discomfort often found in everyday life.

Ongoing brain health, not to mention physical and spiritual health, is aided by participation in recovery programs. Also, there are often potlucks. So that's something.

25

Just When You Think
You Can't Hang on Any More

ONE OF THE PEOPLE I enjoy listening to most in meetings is Ruby. She's been clean and sober about seven years and I've known her since she was brand new. I've watched her go through relationships, her college education, the beginning of a new career, marriage, and the birth of her first child. And I've learned from everything she's had to say about what it's like to live as a sober young woman.

Years ago a young DJ told me that when I spoke I was "droppin' science." I was pleased to discover this was a compliment. Well, Ruby drops some serious science every time she shares.

Ruby, in common with everyone else who is happily clean and sober, takes full responsibility for her addiction and recovery. The adults in her family drank, but not excessively. Even if they had used excessively, she says they weren't "brilliant enough to create alcoholism." She always felt that sense of anxious apartness that seems to be particularly acute in people who become addicts. Ruby describes having serious suicidal feelings starting by age ten and an overwhelming feeling that she missed the course called "Life 101."

In grade seven she and some friends were going through a punk rock phase. They listened to loud, fast music and wore Doc Martens and black clothes. A teacher accused them publicly of being Satan worshippers. The entire experience spiralled out of control, and although the teacher eventually backed off, every kid he'd accused wound up traumatized.

By grade eight, Ruby's grades had gone from A's to barely passing. She was smoking cigarettes and marijuana and drinking what she referred to as "shit mix" (alcoholic concoctions stolen from parents' liquor cabinets). Drinking proved very effective in helping her escape her feelings.

She admits that from a young age she was very attracted to the "dark side." She says she glamorized people who'd had difficult upbringings or were down and out. She was a successful chameleon and could move from group to group, but was happiest with the rocker/drug crowd because she found no judgment there.

At fourteen, she met her first serious boyfriend. He was eighteen and had just been released from jail. Over their three-and-a-half-year relationship, his heroin addiction progressed and he was in and out of several institutions. Ruby says he gave her something to focus on other than herself. She was, she says, "wired to the addict." The year she turned eighteen, her boyfriend died of an overdose. That's when Ruby really began to go downhill, drinking very heavily and doing harder drugs. Her goal was never to be sober.

Her first go at treatment was an outpatient program in Victoria, B.C. She was sent there in lieu of being charged with fraud. She reports leaving the program and going home to get drunk every night. By this time, she was spending time with very serious people: murderers, dealers, and assorted criminals. And she herself was dealing. Every time she got loaded, she would talk about cleaning up. In fact, she says that's all she talked about.

After a long binge during which she couldn't stop drinking or using, despite the fact that the drugs and alcohol weren't providing any relief, she called a crisis line. They told her to go to the hospital.

She did as suggested and begged to be admitted. The hospital sent her home. This incident, she believes, was a huge blessing in disguise. If she'd been taken in and diagnosed with something like depressive disorder or some other label, she might never have sobered up.

Finally, she called her mother, who'd joined Alanon to help her cope with Ruby's disintegration. Twenty-four hours later Ruby was in treatment at Edgewood. Many alcohol and drug programs insist people be clean and sober for a period of time before they can be admitted. Ruby is grateful that Edgewood didn't have any such policy.

At treatment Ruby says she surrendered almost right away. It wasn't hard to admit that her life was a shambles. A few months before entering treatment, she'd found out that she was three months pregnant. She'd been drinking and getting high the whole time and had no idea that she was pregnant. She'd had an abortion. That was what ultimately put her over the edge. "I couldn't believe that I was living a life so polluted that keeping my baby wasn't even a choice."

She spent forty-four days in treatment. When she got out, she went to meetings, but she also picked up with an old boyfriend. She had no clean and sober friends, and to stay busy and "make up for lost time" she started working eighty hours a week.

During a trip home at New Year's, she relapsed. Her plan was just to drink, but as soon as she had a drink, the drugs followed. The slip was, she says, what she needed. She went back to meetings and got honest about not "getting it." Instead of pretending like she had it all together, she would announce, "I don't know what the fuck you people are talking about." She got close to several sober women, let go of her old relationship, eased up on work, and enrolled in a program that helped with the transition back to school and eventually college.

I met her during her "I don't know what the fuck you're talking about" phase and still found her uniquely articulate about the experience of being newly sober. Now she's a magnet for women, young and old, partly because she's funny and well spoken and partly because she's honest. Honesty is definitely an attractive ingredient.

I asked Ruby if she had any advice for people new in recovery and she took a moment to consider. "Tell them that just when you think you can't hang on any more, you can. Even if it's by your fingernails." She paused and added, "Oh, and if you don't put it in your hand, it won't end up in your mouth. The other thing is, happy people don't like to feel nothing. Only for addicts and alcoholics, numb is the goal." In other words, if you don't allow yourself to feel sadness and discomfort, you can be sure you're not going to feel happiness. She pointed out that for those of us who've crossed the line into addiction, "using to block your feelings will take away any chance of ever being happy again." Ruby, whose career brings her into contact with many people on the fringes of society, in particular addicts and alcoholics, asked me to remind people that even those of us who are genetically or environmentally predestined to suffer from addiction can get better. She also pointed to the growing body of research that suggests that although anyone can get clean for a while, only people who have ongoing support stay clean.

She says that when she was new she tried not to think in terms of never using again. Instead she thought about trying to create a life, one piece at a time. Today, she doesn't wear the label of reformed addict/alcoholic. She wants to be judged on her own merits. And they are many.

26

Anonymous, Except to Each Other: AA, NA, and the Other As

AA

Alcoholics Anonymous is the granddaddy of the twelve-step programs. Most people know someone in movies or on T.V. or in real life who is in AA or was; something like three to four million people have gone to at least one AA meeting.*

Then there are the people who used to go to AA. You might have run into one of these in a bar or at a party. Perhaps this person mentioned that AA doesn't work. They are right. AA doesn't work for everyone. Or, in the parlance of AA-types, not everyone works for AA. There are many alternatives to AA, including NA, CA, Rational Recovery, SMART, counselling, therapy, religion, and the ever-popular "doing it on your own." Nevertheless, AA, practised the way it's laid out, has a good success rate for people who embrace it.

This last piece of news was greeted with little enthusiasm by my friend at the Cedars. He'd been able to get his head around going to treatment, but membership in a twelve-step program seemed to him to be an intolerable proposition. Many people coming out of treatment centres feel the same. There's a quip popular in recovery and treatment circles. The patient asks: "How long do I have to go to these meetings?" Answer: "Until you want to."

---

* *The Natural History of Alcoholism Revisited*, page 268.

George E. Vaillant, author of the most rigorous, long-term study of alcoholics ever done, notes that "AA involvement is the only statistically significant predictor of abstinence."* This is why many treatment programs introduce patients to AA and NA and encourage them to keep attending when they are released.

To really understand AA you pretty much have to go. And not just once, either. AA meetings have a few things in common: they are based on the twelve steps (see Appendix 1). "Cross-talk" is not allowed; when people share, others are not supposed to jump in and add their thoughts, criticisms, and insights. Some meetings might involve a small group discussing a topic or some piece of AA literature while seated around a table or in a circle. At "podium" meetings, people are called up to a podium to share. At "speaker meetings," one person tells his or her story for the better part of an hour. Some meetings are "open," meaning that anyone, including non-alcoholics, can attend, and others are "closed" and meant only for those with a desire to get clean and sober.

The main text for AA is a large blue book referred to as the Big Book. It was written in the thirties and includes the basic outline for the AA program. In addition to the Big Book, there are dozens of other books and pamphlets published by the General Service Office of AA. If you want to know how AA works, I recommend attending a few meetings and reading that literature. Keep in mind that some of the literature can sound dated. Other publications are more contemporary.

Here are a few other things you should know about AA. Every meeting is different. The mix of people, the size, and the format of the meeting all contribute to give each a distinct feel. Some

---

*Ibid., page 268.

meetings are very loose and allow discussions of issues other than alcohol and drugs, including eating disorders and other kinds of addictions. At other meetings, talking about anything other than your experiences as they relate to alcohol is seriously frowned upon. Generally "newcomers" or people at their first meetings are warmly welcomed and given a lot of slack. You can usually get a sense of a meeting in the first few minutes, and certainly you'll have a sense of a particular meeting after attending it two or three times. Keep in mind that if you join a meeting, you will help to influence its flavour.

Vaillant points out that "attendance at AA is not usually a hedonistic prescription. Sitting on hard chairs in smoke-filled church basements, drinking bad coffee, and listening to poor sound systems and often poorer speakers several evenings a week can feel more like treating one's wounds with iodine or major surgery than with opiates." (Note to the newcomer: you can't smoke in meetings any more. Sorry.) Nevertheless, with persistence a newly sober member will probably find meetings become not just rewarding but even invigorating.

There are meetings for young people, meetings for women, meetings for men and meetings for gays and lesbians, doctors, and lawyers. There are meetings in prisons, halfway houses, and detox centres. AA is sometimes accused of being a cult. I would agree that there are AA members whose enthusiasm borders on alarming, but I am willing to bet that those members were probably even more alarming when they were loaded.

If the term "cult" bothers you, you will be relieved to hear that AA does not fit the sociological definition. For one thing, there are no authoritarian leaders and there are definitely no charismatic leaders. Also, AA doesn't ask anyone to tithe their money. In fact, it has taken a vow of corporate poverty. People drop money in a basket to cover the group's expenses, like rent and coffee and tea, and to maintain an office where phones are answered. Nobody is getting rich. For more information about how AA works and handles money, see the Twelve Traditions, which are a list of principles governing the operation of AA groups and the AA program as a whole, or look at the literature on how the organization is structured.

AA is said to make suggestions, but it doesn't tell anyone what to do. Well, some people in AA will tell you what to do, but you don't have to listen. No one gets kicked out of AA for not following orders. But AA is an interesting subculture, complete with unspoken ideas about what is acceptable and what is annoying. Here are some hints that were passed along by several people with whom I spoke.

If you are asked to share at a meeting, try not to be a "long talker." Long talkers are, as you might expect, people who consistently talk for too long. Because AA emphasizes sharing and opening up, it can be tempting to go on at length and in tremendous detail. This is perfectly acceptable once in a while, especially if you're having trouble. But if there are twenty people attending a one-hour meeting and you always take up thirty minutes of the available time, people will get irritated with you, although they probably won't say anything (unless they happen to be one of those crusty old-timers who are apt to share their feelings with little inhibition). In other words, don't monopolize the meeting. AA is like the rest of the world: no one wants to listen to someone who loves to hear themselves talk. If you get a reputation for being a long talker, people won't ask you to share.

If you are shy, not being asked to share might seem like a blessing, but it's not. One person I interviewed suggested that people in AA get well in direct proportion to how often and honestly they share. In other words, if you stay clammed up for three years and say "pass" every time anyone asks you to share, no one will get to know you and you won't have had the humbling yet liberating experience of wondering whether you just made an ass of yourself with that story you told about vomiting into a hat at your sister's wedding.

One thing that is prized above all else in AA is honesty. If you are asked to speak in an AA meeting and you don't know what to say, admit that. Try not to "talk a line" or to lie, even though if you're anything like me, those things come naturally. If you're at the stage of early recovery where you realize you don't know yourself, how you feel or what you think, say that. People will relate.

If you attend an AA meeting out in the community while you're in treatment, remember that most of the people in the room are not in treatment, and again, try to talk about your troubles with substances rather than your interpersonal problems with your roommates.

People attending AA meetings are encouraged not to overdo it with the "war stories" or "drunkalogues." These are stories about your addiction that illustrate how incredibly bad-ass you were. Some meetings ask people to "qualify" at the beginning. That doesn't mean that you should go on and on about exactly how much you drank, what you drank, and how many women you nailed when you drank. For example. Too much emphasis on the dirty specifics can trigger people's cravings, and romancing the dragon of addiction is dangerous. Besides, glorifying yourself as an addict–alcoholic is counterproductive and, frankly, a little boring.

The same applies to getting too specific about extremely personal things in meetings. AA meetings feel like safe places to get real, and they are, but you will want to do so in a somewhat general way. If you've committed crimes, it's best not to detail them in meetings. If you have a lot of sexual secrets, same thing. Don't say anything in meetings that could get you arrested. What you say in meetings is supposed to stay in the meeting and most of it will. But you aren't dealing with trained CIA interrogators. There may be the odd leak.

If you are dually addicted (i.e., drugs are part of your story), welcome to the twenty-first century. Drugs are part of almost everyone's story. One treatment centre counsellor I met said that almost everyone going into treatment is poly-addicted. Many people are addicted to whatever happens to be handy. He told me that counsellors have been known to fight over people with a single addiction. Thus, while people in AA introduce themselves as alcoholics, many are also drug addicts. AA emphasizes abstinence from drugs and alcohol, and the only requirement for membership is a "desire to stop drinking." It is also a well-established program with a lot of members who have long-term sobriety, so you may find many people attending whose drug of choice was not alcohol. At some meetings it's considered fine to introduce yourself as an alcoholic/addict. At others, such a statement will be frowned on by grumpy purists. The reality is that AA would be a rather small organization if it limited itself only to "pure" alcoholics.

As for the literature, any time a plan for living is written down, it seems inevitable that some people will want to turn it into dogma and suggest that nothing about the original wording can change. There are people for whom AA's Big Book is a sacred text. For instance, the Big Book, the first edition of which was published in 1939, uses the male pronoun throughout. God is also a "he." There is a chapter addressed to "the wife." The stories at the back of the book have been revised several times to reflect the changing demographics of people in recovery, but the first sections have, so far, been left as is. Not everyone finds this kind of language welcoming. But there are some people in AA who get very excited about any suggestion that the antiquated language might be offputting. They worry about being faithful to "what the founders intended." Fundamentalists of all kinds are tiresome, including ones in AA. If you encounter someone like this, find another meeting or learn to tune the person out—unless you find their approach helpful and decide that fundamentalism is the ticket for you. Ignore the things that bother you and keep an open mind about the rest.

As the most successful self-help program in history, AA has shown that it's getting quite a few things right. And you can be sure that even the most dogmatic person is still rooting for you and would, more than likely, do anything in his or her power to help you stay clean and sober.

Sponsorship

The right sponsor can make a huge difference to people in all stages of recovery, particularly those who are new. That said, many people are reluctant to get a sponsor because it can feel embarrassing and lame to go up to someone you may not know very well and say, "Hey, will you be my special friend?" Horror at the prospect of such vulnerability (and the prospect of rejection) is one of the reasons some of us drank and used drugs in the first place.

It can be tempting to pick the first person you see, like I did. These relationships often work out well. Stars align and we click perfectly with our "impulse" sponsor. If you are afraid of rolling the dice, you can ask people with more sobriety if they could recommend someone.

If you want to take some time and choose your own, here are some of the guidelines people use when choosing sponsors. Do you like the person? If you don't, you're probably not going to call him or her when you get in the weeds. However, if you feel like you don't know what to say to him or her, it might just be a matter of giving it some time. Chances are, you have trouble connecting with lots of people with the full weight of sober consciousness pressing down on you.

Does the person have a reasonably happy and functional life? Or is the person in constant chaos? The person with the calmer life is the better bet. This might sound obvious, but most of us are comfortable with a certain level of drama and instability. The problem with sponsors who live with a lot of turmoil is that they might have trouble focusing on you, since they will be barely keeping their own head above water/out of jail/out of small claims court.

There are exceptions. Everyone runs into trouble now and then. Anyone who's been sober more than six months has probably experienced relationship difficulties or money problems. The people with long-term sobriety that I interviewed suggested that having a sponsee can be a lifesaver in such a situation. In other words, you will also be helping the person who sponsors you.

Try to find a sponsor with a decent length of sobriety (at least two or three years) and find one who is the same sex, unless you are gay, lesbian, or transgendered. Then find someone of a gender that doesn't appeal. Or simply find someone for whom you aren't going to develop a case of the hots. It's easier.

The important point is to find a sponsor who likes you. This sounds basic, but it can be tempting to ask the coolest person in the room. The one with some tenuous connection to Hollywood or the one who drives the nicest car. This is all fine, but won't necessarily lead to the best bond. If you're worried no one will like you, don't be. There *will be someone who likes you.* This revolutionary notion is one of the most amazing things about recovery. There's someone for everyone, or as I've heard people say, there's a wrench for every nut. If you're wondering, ask yourself whether the target greets you warmly. Does he or she seem to genuinely care how you are? Those are good indicators.

Now, it can be difficult to get a handle on these things during a one-hour meeting at which the target may speak only once or not at all. This is where temporary sponsorship comes in. Many treatment centres require patients to find a sponsor in AA or NA before they are discharged. Obviously, you are not going to be able to do the kind of in-depth sleuthing I've talked about here. In that case, you can ask someone with a friendly face to be your "temporary sponsor." A temporary sponsor will be in that role until you find another sponsor. Your temporary sponsor may become your permanent one. (Most people have more than one sponsor over the course of their sobriety.)

How can you tell you have a good sponsor? Does he or she listen? Does he or she offer clear advice when you ask for it? No advice when advice is not sought? Does he seem to be active in recovery? Do you feel like she's on your side? Honest but supportive?

Those are all great things.

Of course, a sponsee has a role to play, too. If you have a sponsor, but never talk to him or her, you are fooling yourself. If you tell your sponsor lies or continue to act in ways that are harmful to you and your recovery, you may find yourself looking for a new sponsor. Sponsors are there to support you in your recovery. They are not financial advisors, relationship counsellors, or doctors.

Advice about matters other than recovery should be taken under advisement.

Sponsorship is basically a special support system between friends who share their experiences with one another. When they go well, sponsor–sponsee relationships can feel touched by magic. The odd and slightly hokey formality of the arrangement is one of its strengths. We are forced to do something that doesn't come naturally and that is to ask for help from another human being rather than turn to a drink or a drug for instant solace.

The God Thing

If you have any familiarity at all with Alcoholics Anonymous or Narcotics Anonymous, you have probably heard that they are "spiritual programs." The twelve steps and the Big Book and NA's literature mention "God" and a "higher power" many times. You may have also heard that "God" can be anyone or anything you like. You can have a Christian, Muslim, or Buddhist conception of god or you can use the fashions of Karl Lagerfeld or a newly sprouted daffodil if you like. The main idea is that you are not in charge of the world any longer. That doesn't mean abdicating responsibility for your life. It means figuring out what you reasonably can and cannot change.

For some people this notion of a higher power can be a difficult one to absorb. However, it is possible to kick yourself quite a bit of room in this department, if you are willing to be flexible. I've met people in recovery whose belief in a higher power is about as vague as the softest wisp of fog and they do just fine. Others have a very strong and well-defined sense of their god and are not shy about talking about it. If you have an open mind, you'll be fine. You had your ass handed to you by your addiction and you need help. If you remain open to what that help might be, you will find something. No one will demand a full accounting from you. "That shit is personal," as one guy I spoke with put it. And it is possible to do the prayer and meditation part of the twelve steps with no clear conception of a higher power. Even the most skeptical person probably believes in nature or a life force that runs through all living creatures. It's not much of a stretch to see that active addiction, with its nihilistic consequences, runs contrary to a life force.

There are plenty of people in recovery who don't believe in a standard conception of a religious god. While doing interviews for this book, I met a Taoist, a Buddhist, a wikkan, and several agnostics. Others make the program itself their higher power.

AA is built on taking leaps of faith. Faith that the program will work, faith that if you get a sponsor, go to meetings, act like you have a higher power, don't pick up a drink or a drug, your life will get better. The contrast between people who are dying of addiction and those same people living full lives after a few years in recovery should be evidence enough that some form of higher power exists.

NA and CA

Narcotics Anonymous is like Alcoholics Anonymous, only for drug addicts. I know, I just finished saying that AA is for drug addicts, too. The reality is that most people today who are trying to get sober have used drugs. Some people find the strict focus on alcohol in AA distracting and want to talk to other people who share their particular addiction experiences.

NA is a younger program than AA and, in some areas, is less well-established. It began in California in the early fifties and grew very slowly. According to the NA website, in 1978 there were "fewer than 200 registered groups in three countries." Today, there are over 25,000 groups in 127 countries.

Like AA, NA emphasizes abstinence, including abstinence from alcohol.

Many cross-addicted people attend both programs because they get something out of each. NA's self-titled "White Pamphlet" describes NA this way:

> NA is a nonprofit fellowship or society of men and women for whom drugs had become a major problem. We … meet regularly to help each other stay clean…. We are not interested in what or how much you used … but only in what you want to do about your problem and how we can help.

Many of the same factors at work in AA, including sponsorship and so forth, are at play in NA as well. And as with AA, NA meetings vary from one to the next. To decide whether NA is for you, attend a few meetings in your area to see which ones you like.

CA refers to Cocaine Anonymous. It began in 1982 and by 1996 had over 30,000 members in twenty countries. Similar to NA, CA's "primary purpose is to stay free from cocaine and all other mind-altering substances, and to help others achieve the same freedom."*

One woman I spoke with had an interesting take on the difference between AA, NA, and CA. She felt that one day there should be one big twelve-step program for all substance abusers. It's an interesting idea but not one likely to be seen any time soon. In the meantime, people can choose whichever program or combination of programs works best for them.

---

*Cocaine Anonymous website: http://www.ca.org/.

27

The Dirty Goldfish

WHEN I ASKED her what pseudonym she'd like to use, she had one ready.

"The Dirty Goldfish," she said.

She said she and a friend had recently been speculating about their spirit animals. Her friend decided hers would be a golden retriever.

"I said I'd be a goldfish swimming around in a bowl filled with shit all day long."

I asked what she meant. "When I was moving around all the time, I left my shit all over the place. Everywhere I went, I left something behind. Now it's all coming back to me, one piece at a time. My whole room is filled with dirty, too-small clothing. And I'm going around and around in circles."

The Dirty Goldfish, or DG, just turned twenty. I first met her when she was fourteen or so and her mom was just getting sober. My overall impression was of a quirky kid. Later, I heard that the DG wasn't doing so well. She'd left school, changed her name (and not to Dirty Goldfish), and begun moving around a lot.

I was extremely pleased when she finally surfaced among some friends of mine. In fact, she's put herself in the middle of a group of sober young women and, whether she sees it or not, her goldfish bowl is more like a sixty-gallon aquarium and she's got all sorts of company in there. I knew I wanted to interview DG for this book.

We went to a local Starbucks. DG ordered an iced tea, and while we were waiting, the barista gigglingly offered her a Misto she'd made by mistake.

When we sat down at our table, barely shielded from the highway by a few straggly cedar shrubs, DG said, referring to the barista, "I made out with her once. In a bathroom at a party."

This, I learn, is part of DG's charm. Spending time with her is like hanging out with a gay, clean and sober, twenty-year-old girl version of Warren Beatty. She's endlessly charming and has had a lot of girlfriends. We go over her history, and she tells me that she was left alone a lot as a kid. "I had an overactive imagination, just to keep myself busy. I used to drink fruit juice out of wine glasses and wear wigs around when I was by myself and pretend to get wasted."

She started smoking at ten and didn't like school much. It didn't help that there was no one around to make her do her homework. DG felt hurt all the time by the lack of attention and felt left out because everyone else had a dad.

She says she always had a best friend whom she'd focus on when her mom wasn't around.

"I got along with everyone in high school," she says. "At least, no one concentrated on making my life bad."

She started drinking at eleven and at first didn't see it as a huge problem. There was a lot of drinking in her family at get-togethers and so on.

At fifteen, she decided she was gay. This is the phrasing she uses. She cut off her hair and came out to her mother. By this time, her mother had sobered up, and the two of them were living in Korea, where her mother was teaching English and saving to go to grad school. DG was also drinking every night, putting out cigarettes on her arms, and cutting herself.

She left Korea on her own after falling in love with a girl she met online. She moved to Vancouver where she started "snorting coke out of rolled-up twenty dollar bills, drinking Baby Duck and Colt 45s. I was living the dream," she says, wryly.

She spent her time in Vancouver moving between friends' and girlfriends' houses. "I'd go to punk rock shows and parties in the park and pick out the person who'd be my saviour for the night," she said. "I'd go to the parents and say, 'I'm this sad-ass kid and I need some help.' That whole time I only had to sleep outside three times."

She burned her bridges with her own family members who took her in. And she began spending more and more time with street kids, panhandling and, on one terrifying occasion, sleeping in a flophouse for meth addicts.

"I locked myself in a room. There were tons of drug addicts in there and mattresses everywhere: at the bottom of the stairs, in the bathroom and the kitchen. You wouldn't believe the noises that night. I was afraid to come out to go to the bathroom."

I asked if she saw any difference between her and the kids who lived on the streets full time.

"They didn't have what I had. People cared about me. Like there was this one girl, Kelsey. And she had her own ideas about what freedom was. She used a sock for a pad. She got pissed on by drunk guys when she slept outside. She could have gotten counselling and help, but she didn't want it."

Another factor was her decision to stay away from crack and meth. She saw what those drugs did to some of the kids on the street and, later, people in treatment and didn't want to know about it, at least not first-hand.

She continued to bounce from place to place. She'd go to Vancouver Island, stay with friends or relatives. When things got uncomfortable, she'd move on. She says there were always girlfriends to catch her.

"Online, I'd be like, 'Hi, I'm DG, I'm a gypsy. I live to get shitfaced.' And they'd invite me to their town."

For a while she stayed with a friend of her mother's and they moved to Mexico. There she drank, smoked weed, and did coke with a family friend who drove a Hummer and liked to have intellectual conversations. She later lived in Edmonton and then back in Vancouver. With every move, things got more out of control.

She talked about working in a restaurant on Robson Street. "Everyone there was on something," she says. "The guy on my right was on ecstasy, the guy on my left had been drunk since two o'clock, and the boss was getting coke delivered to the back door." Her whole life was working, partying, and sleeping.

Pretty soon, the working fell away and it was just using. She and her girlfriend would get up, take a handful of pills, go out and shoplift a Red Bull from Shoppers Drug Mart, and then go downtown to shoplift some liquor. It was during this time that she was jumped by several people after a party and badly beaten up.

"Good times," she says.

She finally called her mother, and the next thing she remembers is finding herself dancing on a speaker at a nightclub in Poland, where her mother was studying. Poland was followed by London, Vancouver, Arizona, back to Mexico, and then Calgary. Finally, she was back on Vancouver Island. "I was an empty shell of a human

being. My big joy was smoking weed in the woodshed out behind the place where I worked." Her mother, who'd come to visit, offered her an ultimatum: You can keep going like this or let me get you some help. By this time, her mother had been clean and sober for six years.

When DG was finally admitted to a local detox centre, she was nineteen and had been sober for five days. From there she went to Athena House, a six-bed house for women in post-acute withdrawal. Here she really got a look at what lay in store for her if she didn't get clean. "There was a murderer in the bunk bed at the end, and a woman who talked in two voices beside me."

Although everyone at Athena was older, she says that pretty soon she started getting excited about life. "Everyone liked me and I was getting along with everyone. It was a safe place. I was there for a month. We did arts and crafts and made collages. I loved it. It was more like a psych ward than a treatment centre."

Then she was transferred to Charlford House, and her recovery got more intense.

"There was the girl popping her blisters and people fighting in the kitchen and people flipping out in group." She wasn't allowed to coast. "I found myself bawling in the arms of a woman who'd lost her kids. I'd felt nothing for five years. I refused to talk about anything. I'd been stealing, lying, and deceiving. And now it was all coming out in front of strangers."

She spent five months in treatment. I asked what was most useful about her stay in treatment, and she says it was a letter she wrote to herself at the age she was before she started using drugs and alcohol. She got to apologize to her younger self for putting her in situations where she got hurt, for having friends who weren't really friends, and for the self-abuse and mutilation.

DG had been out of treatment for a month when we did our interview. She's surrounded herself with women who are active in recovery, and her natural charms have not diminished. As we talk, we overhear two people at the next table. They are obviously discussing recovery. We hear the words "fifth" and "relapse" and we know. When they get up to leave, they come over to DG.

"Hey," says the girl, who looks to be in her early twenties. "We couldn't help but overhear some of what you said. We're in recovery too."

Her friend, a guy around the same age with a crazy haircut, nods. "I've been clean a year."

"Two years," said the girl, pointing to herself.

They shook DG's hand after exchanging names. "It's awesome to meet you. We'll see you around."

DG looks pleased.

I finish by asking if she has any advice for others. "Don't leave," she says. "Just suck it up and listen. And remember that you probably didn't wake up one day and decide your life was perfect and that you should get into recovery."

Oh, Dirty Goldfish, that water's looking clearer every day.

2 8

Doing the Lone Ranger

SO YOU'RE GOING to do it on your own? Well, good luck with that.

Seriously though, some people do quit without help. They are rare.

Not long ago I read a book by a young woman who wrote about her excessive drinking. The book was beautifully written and did a great job of exploring the inner life of the high school and college drinker. This woman and her friends were serious enough drinkers to end up in hospital with alcohol poisoning and to experience frequent blackouts. No namby-pamby little tipplers, these girls. But the book went south for me when, near the end, the young woman decides that society's attitudes toward women in general and advertising in particular had somehow led her into the drinking life. The theory seemed to be that her self-esteem and that of her binge-drinking friends had been so damaged by their cultural environment that they were nearly forced to drink. Her solution was to just say no. She quit cold turkey one fine day and never looked back.

Huh, I thought. *How nice for her.*

The dream that one day we'll up and quit whatever addiction is eating our lives—booze, drugs, food—is a primary obsession of almost every alcoholic and addict, second only to "How do I get more?" For anyone who has turned a corner into genuine drug addiction or alcoholism, that dream of quitting on one's own is unlikely to come true. We've all heard the stories: he just stopped one day. Just like that. We shake our heads, as we would upon hearing that he won the lottery. That lucky bastard!

But the chances of experiencing a spontaneous remission from serious alcoholism and drug addiction are low. If you are merely a heavy user or drinker, it might be possible. But if you've lost the power of choice in your using, you are in serious trouble.

In *The Natural History of Alcoholism*, George Vaillant found certain factors that worked for people who became abstinent on their own:

1   The people found an alternative to their addictive substance, such as alternative substances, compulsive work or hobbies, belief, prayer, or meditation.
2   They developed a serious medical problem that interfered with their using.
3   They got involved in a religious organization.
4   They acquired a new love relationship, either with a romantic partner or a mentor or close friend.

Many alcoholics and addicts reject offers of help and say they'd like to try doing it on their own. One can understand. It reminds me of that old saying, who wants to join a club that would have me as a member? Also, who wants to admit that addiction has you in a bear hug and is eating your face? No one.

The prospect of quietly (and bravely) quitting is so much more attractive. Some of the addiction memoirs that have really taken off in recent years have been those in which, through force of will, the afflicted person has quit without help. Just walked away. Of course, at least one of those memoirs turned out to be fictitious.

I suspect that in addition to the fact that such stories are often over-the-top good yarns, what excites people about them is the notion that addiction can be conquered without help. There are instances in which this happens. There are people in my own family who showed signs of having serious addiction and who, after treatment or a time in a self-help program, dropped out and stayed clean and sober. They now have stable family lives and have had for years. I've seen others cut back and maintain heavy but manageable substance intake. In other words, they are able to work and maintain relationships. They function.

But for those of us who have tried many times to cut down and to quit on our own, the notion that we will one day be able to do this is the dream that keeps us sick. I tried over and over to quit but the minute the opportunity to drink came up, I forgot. *I could not remember not to drink.* I'd be quit. A clean and sober young woman. An upstanding citizen. I'd go out with my friends and ten minutes later I'd be halfway through my third drink and remember: Damn! I was supposed to be quit! Oh well, I'll get to it later.

After a period of recovery, I was given the choice again. Now, if I drink, it will be because I have made a decision to do so. That's what time in a recovery program has given me. The ability to choose. It is the most humane and empowering choice I've ever had. I am allowed to have the dignity to direct my own life.

Getting clean and staying sober with the help of others often requires time in a treatment centre, an aftercare program, ongoing participation in a program such as AA or NA or SMART plus counselling, and a large dose of grace. Getting clean and staying sober using only one's unaided will requires the equivalent of a three-minute submersion in an Olympic-sized miracle pool, a burning bush, and a permanent grace-dispensing IV. Good on you if you can clean up on your own, but if you find it's too hard, the help is available.

Part of the difficulty is the ongoing "living with yourself" piece. Most programs are aimed at helping people who have pre-existing issues or problems caused by drugs and alcohol to exist and function in regular society. This can be particularly challenging for those who start using substances early in life. Most of us didn't hit our personal-development and life-skills milestones. They say people stop maturing when they begin using heavily. That leaves a lot of us emotionally twelve or thirteen years old when we sober up, trying to act like the twenty- or thirty- or forty-year-olds we actually are. Most of us have trouble handling disappointment, pain, discomfort, or any sort of delay in gratification. I had the social skills of a particularly awkward thirteen-year-old. Only time and generous support from other people who were or had been in the same boat helped me cope. I interviewed one beautiful, poised young woman who talked about having one year of sobriety and literally falling on the floor in anguish when she didn't get a job she wanted.

If I'd been left alone with my paranoia, anger, fear, crippling shyness, and the rest, it would have been too hard. Many of the people I spoke with for this book talked about the difficulty of going it alone. One friend told me, "I was crazier sober than I was when I drank. It got to be too much. I couldn't handle it." She decided to join AA when she had already been abstinent for a year and a half.

If you are convinced you can do it alone, fly at it. Get all the knowledge you can and give it a shot. But if you find you can't do it alone or your quality of life and mental state is too harrowing, consider getting some help.

29

Other Forms of Assistance

Rational Recovery

Rational Recovery is, according to its website, "the exclusive, worldwide source of counseling, guidance, and direct instruction on self-recovery from addiction to alcohol and other drugs through planned, permanent abstinence." It was begun in 1986 by Jack Trimpey. Rational Recovery used to offer group meetings, but the program is now offered only via the Internet, books, videos, and lectures.

RR believes that recovery is an event rather than a process. It rejects the disease model of addiction and suggests that those who drink or use too much need to focus on their abilities and reject addictive thinking and thoughts. RR encourages people to follow their "own native beliefs and intuitions" and quit once and for all.

There is much that is interesting on the website, and the program looks as though it could be quite useful, if one can set aside the hostility aimed at other recovery programs, treatment centres, addiction counsellors, and the special loathing reserved for AA.

As noted in the previous chapter, people who sober up without ongoing support are often prone to paranoia and anger issues. At risk of sounding glib, I'd venture a guess that the founder of Rational Recovery could use a meeting. The website rails against "cultural recoveryism" as evidenced by a time when Google "banned" Rational Recovery for a month in 2008.

To join Rational Recovery, people are asked to subscribe to the website or to become a "patron subscriber."

A splinter group called SMART Recovery formed from Rational Recovery when RR stopped holding group meetings. SMART Recovery is an international non-profit that provides help to addicts and alcoholics. It uses a secular, science-based approach, including techniques such as Motivational Enhancement Therapy and Cognitive Behaviour Therapy. SMART offers a four-point approach to recovery: building motivation, coping with urges, problem-solving, and lifestyle balance. It is often listed as an alternative to twelve-step programs, but many people use it in conjunction with the twelve steps.

Counsellors, Doctors, Addiction Specialists

Many addicts and alcoholics use the services of counsellors, therapists, doctors, and addiction specialists. Among counsellors, therapists, and doctors, the degree of knowledge about addiction may vary, as may the preferred approach to dealing with substance abuse issues. In order to access subsidized rehab services, you will in many cases need to be referred by a drug and alcohol counsellor or a doctor.

Professional help can be particularly valuable once a person has achieved a period of sobriety. When people are still using, they tend to create the same problems over and over. People in recovery, on the other hand, have a shot at actually working through their issues, and professionals offer a wide range of supports that cannot be accessed through self-help programs alone.

Harm Reduction

Harm reduction is public health policy aimed at reducing the damage that results from high-risk behaviours, such as substance abuse, casual (unprotected) sex, and the sex trade. According to the International Harm Reduction Association, harm reduction includes "policies and programs that attempt primarily to reduce the adverse health, social and economic consequences of mood altering substances to individual drug users, their families and communities, without requiring a decrease in drug use." The British Columbia Community Guide to Harm Reduction calls harm reduction "a set of non-judgmental policies and programs" and notes that "for some people, abstinence is the most feasible way to reduce harm. Interventions that aim for abstinence and for safer drug use both have a place within harm reduction." On the spectrum of harm-reduction activities, you'll find needle exchange programs, sex education, condoms in schools, methadone programs, and certain types of drug and alcohol counselling.

Harm reduction is controversial in certain quarters because it is seen as condoning unhealthy or immoral activities. Other people point to the evidence that shows that some harm-reduction strategies minimize the damage done to individuals who engage in potentially dangerous activities.

Perhaps the only thing even more insidious than the idea that one day addicts/alcoholics will finally be able to just say no is the idea that they will find that miracle technique that will allow them to start using or drinking "socially." This is also the idea that underlies some harm-reduction programs, particularly those designed for adolescents and low-bottom (severely hard-up) addicts and alcoholics. The thinking seems to be that in the case of teens, they'll grow out of it, and in the case of street people, they *can't* get better.

One nineteen-year-old woman I spoke with who'd gotten sober at seventeen told me about sitting down with her high school counsellor. They worked out a program whereby she would smoke pot only three days a week rather than seven. She would confine her drinking to Fridays and Saturdays, and she would stop getting drunk on school nights. It was a good plan, but not a successful one. Her addiction proceeded unimpeded, and by grade eleven she was in a twelve-step program.

One counsellor I spoke with, who felt that abstinence is the only real solution for addiction, referred to harm reduction as "harm induction." Another treatment expert I interviewed called it "palliative care," and another suggested that harm reduction was promoted by "well-meaning people who do not understand the addicted mind." Those who are skeptical of harm reduction point out that addicts and alcoholics are often obsessed with finding methods that will allow them to continue to use. Other people worry that harm-reduction policies shield the addict or alcoholic from the consequences of their using, which can prolong the disease or even make it impossible for the addict to clean up.

Harm reduction is practised and promoted by numerous in- and outpatient programs and promoted by all manner of counsellors. In Canada, many programs that receive government funding follow the harm-reduction model. When I asked addiction specialists why harm reduction is so popular, they pointed to measurable statistics. You can create statistics, for instance, to show how much crime is being prevented or how many fewer trips to jail a person experiences. Harm reduction certainly has its place.

If you are not ready to quit drinking or using, by all means try a harm-reduction program. If it doesn't work, abstinence is a good thing to consider. Using clean needles may prevent the spread of AIDS, but it's very unlikely to aid in a user's rehabilitation.

30

Family Affair

EVEN FOR THOSE who don't know their story, the three of them intrigue people. A friend once spotted Shane in a coffee shop. Later she whispered, "Hey, is that guy in a band?"

Shane certainly looks like he's in a band (a heavy one, named after a power tool) or at least like the professional motocross stunt rider he used to be. He's got full-sleeve tattoos, is liberally pierced, and wears rolled-up ball caps, black shirts with jagged white lettering, and low riders.

His older brother, Tim, is also imposing, both in his street clothes with tattoos showing and in his business suit. Tim rides a Harley and often wears a slightly bemused "go ahead, try and surprise me" look.

Shane and Tim together are straight-up intimidating. At least, they are until you see them with Dara, Tim's beautiful young wife, or until you hear them speak. They are raw and effective speakers.

Dara, Tim, and Shane are an example of a new kind of young family. They are all young, all clean and sober, and they've built lives and relationships based partly on a shared recovery from devastating addictions.

When I interviewed them for this book, I made the mistake of suggesting that Tim and Dara might be appealing figures to other young people concerned about the inherent uncoolness of sobriety, with all its surrendering and asking for help and so forth. Tim shook his head. He wants no part of that or of being half of "the ideal couple in recovery."

"Too much pressure," agreed Dara.

Tim and Shane grew up without a father, and Tim felt responsible for his younger brother. That didn't stop him from disappearing down the rabbit hole of addiction. Tim is a huge guy, tall and wide-shouldered. He dwarfs Dara on the leather couch in their tidy living room. When the two enormous mastiffs he and Dara own stand near him, they look almost like normal dogs. It's hard to believe that Tim was 130 pounds and covered in chemical sores when he showed up at treatment nine years ago. He was twenty-four years old and had been cycling between jail and the streets for years.

He and Shane started out the way most teens do. It was fun to smoke and drink and get high. In their circle, it was not only socially acceptable, it was socially desirable. Lurking beneath the surface were doubts, however. Both Tim and Shane had learning disabilities and hated school. They ended up on parallel fast tracks to personal destruction.

When Tim's drug use got seriously out of hand, he started dealing and, as he puts it, "doing crime," to get money.

"When did you know you had a problem?" I asked him.

"I don't know, exactly."

Shane jumps in. "How about when you were smoking crack in that security job you used to have—did you see that as a problem?"

Tim laughs ruefully.

Tim graduated from booze and pot to designer and hard drugs and wound up addicted to crystal meth. Rather than being dissuaded by his brother's addiction, Shane also started using the drug on weekends. The brothers would run into each other only in what they called "using places."

Finally, Tim went on a four-day run on crystal and ecstasy. All pretence of socializing was gone. He'd stolen from his mother and used his brother's name after getting caught in a stolen vehicle. He was given a choice between another, much longer, trip to jail and treatment.

He chose treatment. For some reason, he finally saw that the freedom he'd always thought drugs gave him was, in reality, a prison.

Tim spent months in Edgewood, and when he got out, all he really wanted to do was rebuild his relationships with his mother and younger brother. Unfortunately, Shane was so far into his own addiction by this time that it was nearly impossible. Tim would go to see his brother, only to have his own brutal past reflected back at him. His younger brother was living in an unfinished guest house on their mother's property. He had a mattress and not much else.

I asked Shane what, if anything, he noticed about Tim during Tim's early recovery.

"He got big," says Shane. "Then he met this girl with big pipes."

He is referring to Dara. She and Tim met when Tim had been clean and sober for about two years. Dara is very fit (hence the reference to muscular arms) and she's also strikingly beautiful. When Tim met her, she was working at the gym he attended. She was also drinking heavily and was a chronic weed smoker and frequent cocaine abuser. Once she realized that Tim was clean and sober, she hid her use from him, but he wasn't fooled. After they'd been dating for a few months, he told her that his recovery came first and that he wasn't going to endanger it for anyone. She didn't want to lose the relationship so she quit drinking.

At first, Dara thought that getting clean and sober would be easy. She reluctantly went to meetings with Tim for the first year but remained unconvinced that she needed them. She did notice, however, that without alcohol and drugs she was "quite a bit more fucked up" than she'd expected. Dara started getting terribly depressed and even suicidal. After a year, Dara and Tim broke up. She slipped almost immediately. Getting loaded didn't work for her any more, and she decided that she would try recovery for herself. She found her own friends and started attending a women's meeting. Eventually she and Tim got back together.

When Tim had been sober for six years, Shane ended up in the same treatment centre Tim had gone through. Asked what led him to quit, Shane says, "I hated myself. I hated school. I hated work. All around me people were getting married, getting houses, getting things. I had nothing. I tried to commit suicide a couple of times. My family was done with me. Even my buddies I used with were telling me, 'Dude, you're pretty messed up.' I was living in a car with my dog and doing crime for money. But even then I couldn't see it. I'd go to the casino, win some money, get a nice hotel room, and have a party. After a certain situation I saw that I had to do something."

"What situation?" I ask.

"Something I told myself I'd never do. I beat on my girlfriend. And she left me. That was it."

The minute Shane said he was ready to go to treatment, Tim made it happen.

"Dara and I were in a boat in the middle of a lake, and I was working the phone, trying to get him into treatment," he says.

I ask the three of them what it's like being a young, sober family.

"I don't have to be a father figure. Not a caregiver, just a friend," says Tim. "And I had to figure out that what works for me doesn't necessarily work for Dara or Shane."

"We wouldn't be married today if he still thought he had to take care of me," says Dara.

Tim felt responsible for Shane, and when Dara first sobered up he felt responsible for her, too. Finally, he says, he had to "put down that whole bag. Everybody gets to be responsible for themselves." "You can't get away with anything in this family: no bullshit, no behavioural things," says Shane.

Finally, I ask Tim and Shane about how they reconcile the public perception of them. Tim's Harley and Shane's overall look cause people to jump to conclusions. The first conclusion is often that they are drug dealers. Dara talks about the time they all got the stink eye from a group of cops when they pulled up to a local Tim Hortons. It should be noted that they were in Dara's truck, which is enormous and black and looks like she either works for a TV FBI squad or is in a gang. She is also legendary for backing into things with said truck, but that's another story.

Shane says it's all the same to him. Three years of recovery have taught him that you never know who's really suffering. "It could be the rich guy in the suit or the guy off the street."

Tim, who has worked his way up in a local company to become a top manager, struggles with conflicting impulses. "Now I'm a suit and tie guy," he says. "But I don't feel like that's really me." It is the recovery version of an identity crisis.

Shane, who just graduated from college and is preparing to begin his trade as a welder, is closer to the street scene. He recently felt the effects of the gang violence that has been raging on the Lower Mainland. About six months before our interview, Shane and some childhood friends were at a bar when a guy in a hoodie walked in with a gun. The gunman went into the bathroom and killed a young man. Then he turned the gun on a friend of Shane's, who had the misfortune to be standing beside the target. Shane was the one who got to his friend first and held him in his arms as he died. Later, the police treated Shane and his friends like they were gang members, refusing to tell them what hospital their friend had been taken to. Of the group, Shane was the only sober one. He was the one who felt the full brunt.

In the aftermath, Shane has not numbed out with drugs or alcohol, even though he very much wants not to feel.

I ask him how the experience is affecting his recovery.

"I feel brand new," he says. "Lost, lonely. I'm shut down. I don't want to talk. I'm backing off again. I don't want to feel it. But I won't drink over it. That's not the cure."

As soon as Shane got home, he turned to Tim, who had also been friends with the young man who'd been murdered. When Shane talks about the horrifying experience, about his reluctance to feel his anger and helplessness, about the nightmares, and about not knowing how to respond, at the time of the shooting and now, in the aftermath, I see Tim get very still. He listens to his brother with an intensity that is almost palpable. Though they may not realize it, both he and Dara lean imperceptibly toward Shane, as though they can absorb some of the emotion coming off him. As Shane speaks, his pain is evident, but it's also clear to me that he is not alone, and when he's ready to feel, there will be people there to help him get through it, sober.

Appendix 1

Twelve Steps of Alcoholics Anonymous

The steps for other programs, such as NA or CA, are based on these:

1 We admitted we were powerless over alcohol—that our lives had become unmanageable.
2 Came to believe that a Power greater than ourselves could restore us to sanity.
3 Made a decision to turn our will and our lives over to the care of God *as we understood Him.*
4 Made a searching and fearless moral inventory of ourselves.
5 Admitted to God, to ourselves, and to another human being the exact nature of our wrongs.
6 Were entirely ready to have God remove all these defects of character.
7 Humbly asked Him to remove our shortcomings.
8 Made a list of all persons we had harmed, and became willing to make amends to them all.
9 Made direct amends to such people wherever possible, except when to do so would injure them or others.

10 Continued to take personal inventory and when we were wrong promptly admitted it.

11 Sought through prayer and meditation to improve our conscious contact with God *as we understood Him*, praying only for knowledge of His Will for us and the power to carry that out.

12 Having had a spiritual awakening as the result of these steps, we tried to carry this message to alcoholics, and to practise these principles in all our affairs.

Appendix 2

A Slightly Unserious Guide to Recovery-Speak or Don't Leave Because You Don't Understand the Message

Acceptance Often defined by what it's not: it's not bitching, resisting, obsessing, or bargaining. Much easier to talk about acceptance than to do it.

Amends Not just saying sorry, but acting differently, most notably by staying clean and sober.

Behaviours and Isms Refers to inappropriate, addictive, ill-considered actions and thoughts not resulting from intoxication. It's often said that people who don't drink or use may "still have all the Isms." This news is not greeted with delight by the receiver of the diagnosis.

Boundaries Invisible lines between one person and the next. Exist in the emotional realm as well as the asking-for-favours realm. Height and thickness of boundaries depend on person having them. Some people have concrete-wall boundaries. Don't ask those people to help you move. Other people have virtually no boundaries. If someone shows up at your house Sunday morning at 7:30, slips into your favourite bathrobe without asking, and proceeds to spend the next twelve hours talking about his childhood and innermost fears, stopping only to go through your fridge, he may have low/thin/non-existent boundaries. Such a person will also be unusually comfortable with crying in public. If you are concerned about whether you or someone you know might have weak or non-existent boundaries, see: Co-dependence.

Brainwashed What extremely enthusiastic people in recovery are said to be. Traditional rejoinder: some people need a good brainwashing.

Burning Desire This is the time in a meeting when the chairperson asks if anyone who has not been chosen has a desire to share. Someone almost always does. Sometimes the speaker has the desire to speak well into Overtime. Burning-desire shares sometimes give other people burning resentments.

Carrying the Message Telling people in the throes of their addiction that there may be another way. A better way. A way that involves less puking and crime.

Character Defects These are natural instincts run wild, such as the instinct to get more money (drug lords and hedge fund managers); instinct to get more sex (causing rampant thirteenth stepping); and instinct to get more security (glomming onto people and doing things like getting three or four jobs).

Co-Dependence A co-dependent is a person whose happiness and sense of well-being depends entirely on another person. Someone who financially supports and is overinterested in/overconcerned for someone else. If you have an addict girlfriend and she gets busted and you tell the cops the stuff was yours, you are probably co-dependent. If you are an alcoholic and your mom calls your manager at Pizza Hut when you are too hung over to go in and tells them that your mononucleosis has flared up again, then your mom is co-dependent.

Complacency Taking recovery and the life it allows one to lead (presumably a life that has a bit of dignity and personal agency) for granted. Those who get complacent often grow smug and thereby lose Humility and perhaps experience Relapse. When the shit comes down (girlfriend/boyfriend leaves, friends die, jobs are lost), suddenly complacency departs and panic sets in. On the plus side, this gives the aggrieved party the opportunity to decide to recommit to recovery or they can go straight backwards into the pit.

Cult What AA, NA, CA, Overeater's Anonymous (OA), and some other programs based on the twelve steps are assumed to be, much to the annoyance of people in those programs. See also: sudden sympathy for Tom Cruise and Scientology as well as Denial and Resentment and Oversensitivity.

Co-Signing Usually followed by "my/your bullshit." Refers to letting people remain deluded. "Dude, you are totally right that your mom was being an unreasonable snag when she called the police after you stole her jewellery to buy drugs."

Doing What's Suggested Following each program as it's laid out. Getting a sponsor, going to meetings, etc. See also Getting Active.

Drugalugging Pretty much self-explanatory.

Dry Drunk A person who is sober but doesn't go to a Program or get any help. The condition is characterized by a certain savagery of outlook and a tendency to get deep into other Behaviours and Isms. See George W. Bush.

God Quite a multifarious character among recovery types.

Characterized by a certain loving quality and propensity to forgive saints and assholes alike.

Growing in Recovery/Getting Active   In twelve-step circles, this means Doing What's Suggested: working the steps, reading the literature, going to meetings, doing Service, speaking with one's sponsor, Reaching Out. Getting Active is the opposite of Getting Complacent.

Grouped   To be ganged up on by fellow recoveries to uncover your bullshit. Fortunately, not as violent as it sounds.

Half Measures   Not trying very hard. May result in relapse.

Hitting Bottom   Connected to well-loved phrases such as being "sick and tired of being sick and tired." The only requirement for hitting bottom is to decide one has had enough of drinking/using. For some people, the bottom arrives the day they speak injudiciously at the faculty party. For others, the bottom comes when they find themselves in jail for the fourth time. The thing about bottoms is that you have to have hit one to know what it is, and only you get to say when enough is enough.

Inventory   Complete list of personal qualities, good and bad. Unlike in retail environment, most people don't want any help with their inventories. In fact, if you take someone else's inventory, you will cause resentments. That said, just about everyone enjoys taking everyone else's inventory, at least silently.

Issues   Personal problems that annoy other people and make life difficult for sufferer of Issues.

Judge   The sort of person who takes other people's inventory. Can also mean to form an opinion, most likely without all the facts.

Letting Go   Blanket concept applied to old friends, old hangouts, old ideas, misconceptions, delusions, resentments. Closely related to Hitting Bottom and Acceptance.

Long Talker   Someone who speaks for a very long time at meetings, thereby preventing anyone else from getting a word in. See also Resentments, as well as Principles and Not Personalities.

Newcomer   Refers to length of time a person has been in recovery. In some circles you are a newcomer for about a month. Other circles, you'll be a newcomer until you take your twenty-year cake.

Old-Timer   Someone who has been sober for a long time. It's possible to be an old-timer before you are actually old. Something for all those ten-year-olds who are dabbling to consider.

Outside Issues   Serious issues other than drug and alcohol addiction. These may include eating disorders, gambling, mental health problems, serious relationship or financial difficulties, dealing with a history of abuse, etc. Many Outside Issues are best dealt with using Outside Help, in the form of counsellors, therapists, and physicians.

Outside Help   Help provided by professionals rather than lay people in recovery.

Out There   Where people are said to be when they are using. The opposite of "in here" or "in these rooms," which refers to the sober world.

Overtime   When meetings go over the prescribed hour or hour and one-quarter. Hints that you may be going into overtime: people begin shifting in their seats, picking up and opening purses and wallets, muttering, leaving.

Powerlessness   Not to be confused with dependency or helplessness. Powerlessness is an honest, realistic reckoning of what a person can and cannot do through force of unaided will. Things most addicts cannot do include control amount of using, frequency of using, and idiotic, self-destructive behaviour resulting from using; change weather by complaining about it; change people by resenting them and taking their inventory.

Principles and Not Personalities   Pretty much what it sounds like. People are often annoying. Principles are not.

Program   Generally refers to one of the As: AA, NA, CA, OA, etc.

Reaching Out   Calling people in recovery even if you don't know them. Approaching people at meetings and asking if they want to have coffee. Like Acceptance, much harder than it sounds.

Relapse   Drinking or using again after a period of trying to get sober. See also: Shitty Idea and Research.

Research   Going out drinking or using in order to prove to yourself that you are, as you suspected, an alcoholic or addict. Warning: too much Research has been known to lead to death.

Resent/Resentment   The number one killer of alcoholics and addicts. Forming resentments and hanging on to them is one area in which the addictive personality tends to shine.

Service   Helping out those who are new or Still Suffering. Helping out at the group level by chairing meetings, cleaning up after, setting up before, or holding service position for larger area. Listening. Attending meetings.

Still Suffering   People in the throes of their addiction.

Stinking Thinking   Harbouring anger and resentments. Maybe even nurturing them and building them a little blanket fort in your mind and feeding them cookies and petting them so they'll grow. To be avoided. See also: Letting Go and Relapse.

Take a Cake/Take a Chip Celebrating lengths of sobriety with cake, and chips (also known as tokens) and telling the story of one's addiction and recovery. Happens on the occasion of recovery birthdays. May involve actual cake and chips, unless the program is Overeaters Anonymous. Then there will be carrot sticks and low-fat dip.

Thirteenth Step When a person who has been clean and sober for a while helps another person who is new in recovery right out of his/her pants.

Two Stepping Doing only step one (Powerlessness) and step twelve (the Carrying the Message part). Carefully avoiding Amends and other unpleasantness.

Winners People who stay clean and sober or at least try really hard to do so. There are no losers, exactly, but the person who is still wetting his/her own pants at parties is considered a bit less of a winner.

Bibliography

BOOKS

Addiction: Why Can't They Just Stop? Edited by John Hoffman and Susan Froemke. HBO, Rodale and Melcher Media, 2007.

A Natural History of Alcoholism Revisited by George E. Vaillant. Harvard University Press, Cambridge, Massachusetts, 1995.

Beautiful Boy: A Father's Journey Through His Son's Addiction by David Sheff. Houghton Mifflin, New York, 2008.

Drinking: A Love Story by Caroline Knapp. Bantam Dell, New York, 1995.

Dry: A Memoir by Augusten Burroughs. Picador, New York, 2004.

Teens Under the Influence: The Truth About Kids, Alcohol, and Other Drugs—How to Recognize the Problem and What to Do About It by Katherine Ketcham and Nicholas A. Pace, MD, Ballantine Books, New York, 2008.

The Recovery Book by Al J. Mooney, Arlene Eisenberg, and Howard Eisenberg. Workman Publishing, New York, 1992.

Tweak: Growing Up on Methamphetamines by Nic Sheff. Simon and Schuster, New York, 2008.

OTHER RESOURCES

Alcoholics Anonymous: www.aa.org

Association of Recovery Schools: www.recoveryschools.org

Canadian Drug Rehab Centres: www.canadiandrugrehabcentres.com

Cocaine Anonymous: www.ca.org

International Harm Reduction Association: www.ihra.net

Narcotics Anonymous: www.na.org

Rational Recovery: http://rational.org/index.php

SMART Recovery (Canada): www.smartrecovery.ca

SMART Recovery (U.S.): www.smartrecovery.org

U.S. Drug Rehab Centers: www.usdrugrehabcenters.com

Acknowledgments

I COULD NOT and would not have written this book without the help and encouragement of many people. First, Bill Juby, who read it over and over and helped to make it better every time and who showed the way; Mary Madsen and Stephanie Dubinsky, who gave great suggestions; O.R.M., Paul F., Anna S., and my agent, Hilary, who fielded the panicky calls; Barbara Berson, who got the ball rolling; Nicole Winstanley and Jennifer Notman at Penguin for taking such care with the manuscript and making excellent suggestions; Wendy Thomas for her careful copy-editing; Jerry Blackburn at Edgewood Treatment Centre in Nanaimo, Neal Berger at Cedars in Cobble Hill, and Sue Donaldson from Pegasus Recovery Solutions, for their time and generosity and insights into addiction. Thanks also to the dozens of people who shared their stories so honestly for this book and the millions of people who support each other as part of their own recovery. Gratitude to my mom, my brothers, and my aunts, uncles, and cousins, and to my dear Jimmy: best husband in the world. Finally, I could not have written this or any other book without the help of Heather, Kristine, Grace, Sophie, Gail, and Mary and all the other women who have carried me when I couldn't walk, as well as my beloved lucky bitches. We are indeed the lucky ones.